The New York Times

LOOKING FORWARD

Earth 2.0

THE SEARCH FOR A NEW HOME

THE NEW YORK TIMES EDITORIAL STAFF

Published in 2019 by New York Times Educational Publishing
in association with The Rosen Publishing Group, Inc.
29 East 21st Street, New York, NY 10010

First Edition

The New York Times
Alex Ward: Editorial Director, Book Development
Phyllis Collazo: Photo Rights/Permissions Editor
Heidi Giovine: Administrative Manager

Rosen Publishing
Megan Kellerman: Managing Editor
Michael Hessel-Mial: Editor
Greg Tucker: Creative Director
Brian Garvey: Art Director

Cataloging-in-Publication Data
Names: New York Times Company.
Title: Earth 2.0: the search for a new home / edited by the
New York Times editorial staff.
Description: New York : New York Times Educational Publishing,
2019. | Series: Looking forward | Includes glossary and index.
Identifiers: ISBN 9781642821314 (library bound) | ISBN
9781642821307 (pbk.) | ISBN 9781642821321 (ebook)
Subjects: LCSH: Extrasolar planets—Juvenile literature. |
Habitable planets—Juvenile literature. | Life on other planets—
Juvenile literature.
Classification: LCC QB820.E378 2019 | DDC 523.2'4—dc23

Manufactured in the United States of America

On the cover: An artist's rendering of Kepler-452b, the first near-
Earth-size planet orbiting in the habitable zone of a sun-like star;
NASA/Ames/JPL-Caltech/T. Pyle.

Contents

CHAPTER 2

National Space Programs Evolve and Compete

CHAPTER 3

Privatizing Space: The Profit Motive Goes Off-World

CHAPTER 4

New Views of the Solar System

Improvements in space telescopes have allowed for more fine-tuned searches, allowing the discovery of hundreds of planets in the "habitable zone" where liquid water may allow life to flourish. While we have yet found no evidence of life outside of Earth, we've learned more about how it may occur, how solar systems form and the most common types of planets.

While researchers have enjoyed a golden age of exoplanet exploration, developments on Earth and in our solar system have been significant. While NASA remains the largest space agency in the world, leading in technological development, it has seen competition from emerging powers and for-profit space enterprise. Emerging powers such as China and India have developed their space programs to build national prestige. Meanwhile, companies SpaceX and Blue Origin, founded by Elon Musk and Jeff Bezos respectively, have shifted space enterprise from the earlier "space tourism" model to developing technology and services for public space agencies. While these

An artist's rendering that shows the sweep of the NASA Kepler mission's search for planets within the habitable zone.

changes are rooted in national competition and the search for profits, space research remains a work of international cooperation, sharing information and expertise. This work has led to the European Space Agency landing a probe on a comet, the burgeoning Indian Space Research Organization successfully launching a Mars probe on its first attempt, and the discovery of methane on one of Saturn's moons, Enceladus — a possible sign of life.

As diverse fields of space research expand and converge, one planet maintains its hold on the public imagination: Mars. The so-called Red Planet's habitability has been a source of speculation for centuries, and many dream of one day living there. On both of those fronts, we have moved closer. SpaceX founder Elon Musk asserts that the long-term plans for his rocket technology involve sending space colonists to Mars, while researchers examine how the planet's iron-rich soil might accommodate agriculture. More concretely, the newest generation of Mars rovers have discovered evidence of flowing liquid water, which may host microbial life. If life exists on Mars, the next decade's explorations may have the tools to discover it.

The search for Earth 2.0, like other space research, invites skepticism. Why waste resources to find a habitable planet trillions of miles away when there are so many pressing issues on our own planet? Some of those views also appear in this book, as a part of the broader conversation about what Earth 2.0 means in the context of a warming planet and growing social inequality. As other reflections in this book demonstrate, the exploration of our universe — by telescope, by space probe and by terrestrial laboratory research — helps us better understand our own planet and the life it fosters.

CHAPTER 1

A Golden Age of Exoplanet Research

In 1995, exoplanet 51 Pegasi b was discovered — the first confirmed planet orbiting a star like our own. By the middle 2010s, space telescopes like Kepler had discovered thousands of widely varying exoplanets: "hot Jupiters," "super-Earths," "mini-Neptunes" and others that revealed new rules for the formation of solar systems. With them, the occasional habitable Earth-sized planet raised questions: Does life exist there? Could humans visit? While both questions remain unanswered, these discoveries raised the profile of space research.

In a Golden Age of Discovery, Faraway Worlds Beckon

BY JOHN NOBLE WILFORD | FEB. 9, 1997

STANDING OUTSIDE the dome of Lick Observatory on this lofty summit, two astronomers gazed beyond the foothills to the far horizon where California meets the Pacific Ocean. As the solid world at their feet rotated east, the great red sphere of glowing hydrogen seemed to sink perilously close to a doomsday collision, only to slip harmlessly out of sight in the west.

At the moment of sunset, birds somewhere in the trees broke into song, life sounding retreat at the loss of light. The astronomers turned back to the dome and the telescope within. Time to go to work, time to search the heavens for other stars not unlike the Sun and see whether some of them also have companion worlds — other places where night follows day, where there might be air and water, mountains and shore, even life and song.

The two astronomers, Dr. Geoffrey W. Marcy and Dr. R. Paul Butler of San Francisco State University, began another night of work at Lick Observatory, near San Jose, Calif., with the quiet confidence of professionals at the top of their game. In little more than a year, they and other teams in this country and Switzerland have for the first time detected planet-size objects — at least eight confirmed, and possibly two more — orbiting other stars like the Sun.

Even if a few skeptics still question whether these objects, called exoplanets, qualify as true planets, Dr. Alan P. Boss, a theoretical astrophysicist at the Carnegie Institution of Washington, expressed the prevailing view: "I truly believe we have indeed identified the first extrasolar planets."

All of a sudden, astronomers have turned a big corner and glimpsed in the dim light of distant lampposts a universe more wondrous than they had previously known. Other worlds are no longer the stuff of dreams and philosophic musings. They are out there, beckoning, with the potential to change forever humanity's perspective on its place in the universe.

Although no likely habitable planets beyond the solar system have been detected so far, the discoveries, coupled with fresh evidence of the possibility of early life on Mars, have already renewed enthusiasm in the search for extraterrestrial life. The first of a fleet of spacecraft and robotic landers took off late last year to resume Mars exploration. Space telescopes being planned for the next decade should be able to see planets as small as Earth elsewhere and examine their atmospheres for signs of life.

More powerful telescopes on the ground and in space, especially the Hubble Space Telescope, and more sensitive electronic detection instruments are sharpening the view of the cosmos for other astronomers as well. Every few weeks brings more spectacular pictures from the depths of space, pictures of the moons of Jupiter, the nurseries of newborn stars and the galaxies taking shape when the universe was young. They embolden cosmologists, the historians of the universe, in the audacious belief that many answers to questions of cosmic origin and evolution may be within their grasp.

Little wonder scientists today feel justified in proclaiming this to be a new golden age of astronomy.

In that spirit, Dr. Marcy and Dr. Butler were now setting their sights on more planetary discoveries. Among the billions of galaxies, Earth's own Milky Way galaxy alone is populated with 100 billion stars, and a few hundred of these stars are close enough — less than 100 light-years away — to be in range of technology's new gifts of vision, making it possible to detect large planets there.

In the dark control room below the 120-inch Lick telescope, the two astronomers studied the light of target stars as they appeared, one by one, on a video screen. It is slow, tedious work. They were looking for faint variations, no more than 1 part in 100 million, in the frequencies of starlight, betraying the wobbling motions of a star caused by an unseen gravitational force nearby, something the size of a Jupiter or several Jupiters.

There could be no thought of an instant cry of "Eureka!" Hours of computer analysis and months of repeat observations precede any announcement of the discovery of one of these objects, which astronomers are calling extrasolar planets, or exoplanets. But in the wee hours, the two men reflected on the exhilaration of being young on a mountaintop on the only planet known to harbor life and having a part in discoveries with transforming implications.

Dr. Butler, who is 35, remembered the morning just over a year ago when he was "completely blown away" by the realization that a computer analysis showed that an object more than six times the mass of Jupiter was orbiting close to the star 70 Virginis, 80 light-years away. He could imagine the greats of astronomy nodding in awe. "I really felt the presence of Kepler standing at my shoulder," he said.

Professionally, Dr. Marcy, 42, mused, "for us this is the best that will be, at our young ages."

And the discoveries may be only beginning. One recent study suggested that planets might be lurking around half the Milky Way's stars. Astronomers have already seen enough to suspect that their definition of planets may have to be broadened considerably to encompass the new reality. As soon as they can detect several planets around a single star, they are almost resigned to finding that the Sun's family, previously their only example, is anything but typical among planetary systems.

THE QUEST
Seeking Worlds Around the Stars

The Epicurean philosophers of classical Greece would probably not have been surprised by such a turn of events. They believed that the chance conglomerations of infinite atoms in an infinite universe must form "innumerable worlds." Metrodorus of Chios, a disciple of Epicurus, wrote, "It would be strange if a single ear of corn grew in a large plain or were there only one world in the infinite."

When the Polish scholar Copernicus determined in the early 16th century that Earth orbited the Sun, a revolutionary idea began to take root in modern Western thinking: Earth might not be the center of the universe or even unique as an abode of life. Acceptance of that idea was grudging. Giordano Bruno was burned at the stake in 1600 for, among other things, the heresy of speculating about other inhabited worlds.

More recently, scientists have been encouraged in the search for other worlds by the recognition that the laws of physics appear to be universal and that life is a phenomenon based on natural chemical processes that need not be confined to one planet around one rather ordinary star. Since the 1960's, a few radio astronomers have been patiently listening to the heavens, seeking signal patterns that just might come from intelligent extraterrestrials.

Prospects for finding worlds around other stars improved substantially in the 1980's. Dr. Bradford A. Smith, of the University of Arizona

As it turned out, astronomers using radiotelescopes, not spectroscopy or astrometry, were the first to strike pay dirt in the search for planets, in 1994.

Dr. Alexander Wolszczan, a radio astronomer at Pennsylvania State University, reported detecting two and perhaps three planet-size objects orbiting a star in the Virgo constellation. He called this "a final proof that the first extrasolar planetary system has been unambiguously identified."

Although scientists accepted this assessment, they were nonetheless disappointed. Dr. Wolszczan seems to have found planets, but not planets around a normal star like the Sun. They are companions of a pulsar, a dense, rapidly spinning remnant of an exploded star, its thermonuclear furnace dead. The detections were made by observing regular fluctuations in the pulsar's rapid radio signals, indicating the planets' complex gravitational effects on the dead star.

But a pulsar is no place for supporting life. The environment there would lack warming starlight and be saturated with deadly radiation.

Meanwhile, other astronomers were busy studying the visible light of nearby stars for telltale variations of their radial velocity, with no success. Dr. Marcy and Dr. Butler had been at the task since 1987. A group at the University of British Columbia in Vancouver, led by Dr. Bruce Campbell and Dr. Gordon A. H. Walker, who pioneered the spectroscopic search technique, had been looking even longer. Discouraged, the British Columbia group abandoned its fruitless work in April 1995, just before two Swiss astronomers scored the breakthrough.

THE COMPETITION
The Unexpected and a Jump-Start

On Oct. 6, 1995, Dr. Michel Mayor, of the Geneva Observatory in Switzerland, announced that he and a colleague, Dr. Didier Queloz, had discovered a planet orbiting a star similar to the Sun, 51 Pegasi, about 40 light-years away.

The planet has more than half the mass of Jupiter, at least; since the radial-velocity technique can determine only an object's minimum size, the planet's mass could be some 10 times as great as that listed. And, to the surprise and puzzlement of astronomers, the planet is closer to its parent star than tiny Mercury is to the Sun.

At first, astronomers were wary, but the Swiss astronomers had checked their data with care. Dr. Mayor said they had repeated the observations and had also ruled out the possibility that the light variations were caused by the star's pulsations or eruptions like sunspots. When a theorist ran simulations showing that such a large planet could survive intact that near its star, Dr. Mayor decided to go public with the results.

Dr. Marcy and Dr. Butler raced to Lick Observatory to check it out. Yes, a planet was there. They had been scooped, Dr. Marcy said, in part because they had been looking in the wrong place, not expecting that such a large planet could be so close to its star. Their expectations were influenced by the one planetary system they knew well, in which the giant Jupiter, 317.8 times as massive as Earth, is half a billion miles out from its star.

"Mayor jump-started us," Dr. Butler remarked while beginning the night's work on the mountain. "His discovery brought a level of excitement to the field so that we were able to get more computational time and more telescope time. His discovery told us 'Jupiters' could orbit in close. We've each been able to confirm the other's results."

In astronomy, as in anything else, having a clearer idea of what to look for can improve the odds of success. Dr. Marcy and Dr. Butler took another look at their old data on 120 stars and conducted new observations. By a year ago, they had two more planets to report: the one around 70 Virginis, in the constellation Virgo, and another around 47 Ursae Majoris, in the Big Dipper.

More discoveries followed. They detected a planet around Tau Bootis and another around Rho Cancri. In October, Dr. William D. Cochran of the University of Texas at Austin and the Marcy-Butler

Dr. David C. Black, director of the Lunar and Planetary Institute in Houston, is especially outspoken in his belief that most of the objects will prove to be brown dwarfs. One discovery, first thought to be an exoplanet, has been revealed to be a brown dwarf companion to the star Gliese 229.

Dr. Black contends that it is "a bit hasty" to conclude that the objects around 51 Pegasi and 70 Virginis are planets and not brown dwarfs. If these are Jupiter-class planets, he said, they should be in more circular orbits farther out from their central stars, as is the rule in the solar system.

A study directed by Dr. Douglas N. C. Lin, of the University of California at Santa Cruz, yielded a possible explanation for finding actual planets in such cozy proximity to their stars: they could have formed farther out and then migrated inward to their observed positions. "The planet spiraled slowly but relentlessly toward the star," Dr. Lin said. "Finally, inward and outward forces on the planet's orbit canceled each other out just before the star would have consumed the planet."

Dr. Frederic A. Rasio, an astrophysicist at the Massachusetts Institute of Technology, approached the problem by assuming that relatively stable planetary systems like the Sun's, with its one dominant massive planet — Jupiter — may be extremely rare. Assume, instead, that many systems start with two Jupiter-size planets in fairly close proximity. In computer simulations, Dr. Rasio and a student, Eric B. Ford, showed that the strong gravitational interaction between the two planets could lead to one casting the other out of the entire system, while the survivor headed into a smaller orbit or sometimes crashed into the star.

One implication of this model, Dr. Rasio noted, is that any smaller Earthlike planets "are likely to be lost as a result of the instability." They either escape from the system or collide with the central star. Such a violent history could thus preclude the evolution of advanced life in such systems. By the same token, having only one Jupiter may have been a necessary condition making the solar system sufficiently stable for the evolution of intelligent life.

Dr. Black is skeptical of such explanations. "There is one other possibility, namely that planet hunters have discovered a new class of objects," he said.

Only when astronomers discover more than one planet candidate around a single star will they learn if what they are seeing are indeed planets and if other planetary systems bear much resemblance to the Sun's family. For all theorists know now, the solar system could be, as Dr. Marcy said, "the odd bird in the zoo."

THE NEW PROJECTS
'Goldilocks Orbits' Are Just Right

At a workshop where astronomers discussed new ideas for finding exoplanets, someone asked when would be the earliest anyone might begin detecting objects the size of Earth or Mars orbiting other stars at distances comparable to Earth's from the Sun. Scientists call this habitable zone the "Goldilocks orbit," where conditions should be neither too hot nor too cold but just right for life. Without hesitation, Dr. William J. Borucki, of the Ames Research Center in Mountain View, Calif., replied, "2001."

Dr. Borucki's optimism was based on a proposal by him and his colleagues for sending a small satellite into space to focus its telescopic electronic camera on thousands of stars considered to be prime candidates for planetary formation. The instrument should be able to detect a faint drop in the light intensity of a star, suggesting that a planet is passing across its face.

If the project wins Federal approval in the next few months, the spacecraft, called Kepler, could be launched in March 2001; within a few weeks, it could detect some 2,400 new planets, including perhaps 100 that might have a size and solid surface like Earth's.

A more ambitious concept is being developed by Dr. J. Roger P. Angel and Dr. Neville J. Woolf of the University of Arizona. They propose putting a large infrared telescope in deep space that would be capable of detecting the radiated heat of exoplanets. The emissions take another year of observations to be sure. Not a bad ratio, though too soon for observing astronomers to relax and leave their discoveries of other worlds to the meditations of philosophers.

"It's taken a long time getting good at this," Dr. Butler said. "Now I just want to find more planets."

Astronomers Find Earthlike Planet, but It's Infernally Hot

BY KENNETH CHANG | OCT. 30, 2013

KEPLER 78B, a planet some 400 light-years away, is like hell on earth.

Astronomers described it on Wednesday as the first Earth-size planet that seems to be made of the same mixture of rock and iron as Earth, and that orbits a star similar to our sun.

But Kepler 78b would not be a pleasant place to visit. It whirls around its parent star, Kepler 78, at a distance of less than a million miles, and its year — the time it takes to complete one orbit — is just eight and a half hours. (By contrast, Earth is 93 million miles from the sun and, of course, completes its yearly orbit in a little over 365 days.)

At that close proximity, the surface of Kepler 78b is infernally hot: 3,500 to 5,000 degrees Fahrenheit, or "well above the temperature where rock melts," said Andrew W. Howard, an astronomer at the University of Hawaii and the lead author of one of two papers being published in the journal Nature. "This is probably one of the most hellish planets that have been discovered yet."

Viewed from the surface of Kepler 78b, its star would cover 80 times more of the sky than the sun does in Earth's sky.

"It's certainly not a habitable planet," said Francesco Pepe, a professor of astronomy at the University of Geneva and the lead author of the other Nature paper.

Kepler 78b is the newest addition to the pantheon of oddball planets in the Milky Way. The first planet discovered around another sunlike star turned out to be about the size of Jupiter, but orbiting its star at what seemed to be an impossibly close orbit. Other discoveries over the years include a fluffy planet with a density less than that of cork and a planet blacker than coal.

"Exoplanets are just surprising us with their diversity," said Dimitar D. Sasselov, a professor of astronomy at Harvard and a member of Dr. Pepe's team, using the name for planets outside our solar system.

Kepler 78b is one of more than 150 planets spotted by NASA's Kepler spacecraft, which noted the dimming of the starlight when a planet passed in front.

Those findings were published in August. But while Kepler can determine exoplanets' size and orbit, it cannot measure their mass. For that, two teams of astronomers looked at Kepler 78b star from Earth. Dr. Howard's team used the Keck 1 telescope in Hawaii; Dr. Pepe's team used a telescope in the Canary Islands. They could not directly see the planet, but they could spot undulations in the frequency of light from the star caused by the gravitational pull of the planet. The heavier the planet, the larger the swings in frequency.

The teams coordinated their work, agreeing to publish their results at the same time, but they did not collaborate. They decided that they would not exchange their data and answers until their papers were almost complete so that each would serve as an independent check on the other.

In the end, the two teams came up with nearly identical answers. The density of Kepler 78b is 0.2 pounds per cubic inch, the same as Earth's, suggesting that the two planets' makeup is very similar — an iron core with rocky, if melted, outer layers.

"It's the first really well measured Earthlike composition for a rocky extrasolar planet," said L. Drake Deming, a professor of astronomy at the University of Maryland who was not a member of either team but wrote an accompanying commentary for Nature. That astronomers have already found an Earthlike planet suggests that there should be others in cooler, more life-friendly orbits. "You can reasonably conclude from that that it's not rare, because you've found it pretty easily," he said.

That still leaves a mystery: how Kepler 78b got where it is. "Right now, we have no clue," Dr. Sasselov said.

It could not have formed there, because the star as a youngster would have extended into its orbit. A near-miss with another planet could have flung it toward the star, but in that case its orbit would have been elliptical, not circular. Or it was nudged inward by the material that formed the planets.

Another possibility is that it was originally a gas giant like Saturn and that as the planet spiraled in toward the star, all of the gases were stripped away, leaving just the rocky core at the center.

"Right now, this scenario doesn't work, either," Dr. Sasselov said. "If you want me to choose out of four bad ones, that's probably the one which seems least so."

Solar Systems With Their Own Rule Books

BY DOUGLAS QUENQUA | OCT. 9, 2014

IN OUR SOLAR SYSTEM, smaller planets like Mercury and Venus orbit the sun closely, while larger ones like Jupiter tend to be farther away. But other solar systems don't play by our rules.

Large planets that orbit their stars very closely — some at one-tenth the distance between Earth and the sun — are known as hot or warm Jupiters (so named because they have a mass similar to Jupiter's). And unlike the planets in our solar system, some of these planets have unusually elliptical orbits.

Researchers at the University of California, Berkeley, set out to discover how warm Jupiters came to orbit their stars so closely, and whether the answer had something to do with their elliptical orbits.

The researchers ran more than 1,000 simulations to observe the movements of warm Jupiters relative to the other planets in their solar systems.

They found that large planets orbiting farther away were able to drive the large inner planets toward their stars: The planets' surprisingly sharp orbital angles — about 35 to 65 degrees relative to one another — allow them to exert gravitational force on their companions.

"We sort of naïvely expected all planets to be like our solar system in that they are all orbiting in the same plane as each other," said Rebekah Dawson, lead author of the study, which was published in the journal Science. "So to find that there's this population of planets that have a very significant difference in their planes is surprising."

The Telescope of the 2030s

BY DENNIS OVERBYE | JULY 13, 2015

IN WHAT THEY TERMED "a call to arms," an organization of American university astronomers said last week that NASA should begin planning now to launch a sort of supersize version of the Hubble Space Telescope in the 2030s to look for life beyond Earth.

This High Definition Space Telescope would be five times as big and 100 times as sensitive as the Hubble, with a mirror nearly 40 feet in diameter, and would orbit the sun about a million miles from Earth.

Such a telescope, the astronomers said, would be big enough to find and study the dozens of Earthlike planets in our nearby neighborhood. It could resolve objects only 300 light-years in diameter — the nucleus of a small galaxy or a gas cloud on the way to collapsing into a star and planets, say — anywhere in the observable universe.

The case for the telescope is laid out in "From Cosmic Birth to Living Earths," a report on the future of astronomy commissioned by the Association of Universities for Research in Astronomy (AURA), which runs the Hubble and many other observatories on behalf of NASA and the National Science Foundation. It was written by a committee headed by Sara Seager of the Massachusetts Institute of Technology and Julianne Dalcanton of the University of Washington.

"We hope to learn whether or not we are alone in the universe," said Matt Mountain, the president of AURA and the former director of the Hubble, at a news conference at the American Museum of Natural History.

Only once in the arc of our species, Dr. Mountain said, will we turn a corner and be able to determine how the universe and our planet were formed and whether we are alone. "We can be that generation," he said.

But only if we start now.

In releasing the report, the AURA group is putting down a marker in the long, elaborate and very political process by which major scientific projects are chosen and funded. Every 10 years, a committee of the National Academy of Sciences surveys the astronomical community and produces a prioritized wish list for the next decade. This survey, which happens next in 2020, serves as a blueprint for Congress and NASA.

AURA has done this before. Back in 1995, the organization put out a report, led by Alan Dressler of the Carnegie Observatories, calling for a space telescope to succeed the Hubble. That became the James Webb Space Telescope, designed to look for the first stars and galaxies in the universe, and it is on target for launching in 2018, 23 years later.

"In the modern era," Dr. Mountain said, "only space scientists are this patient."

But the cost of the Webb telescope swelled from an initial budget in 1996 of $1.6 billion to nearly $9 billion, acting like a wrecking ball to the rest of NASA's space science budget. To avoid retracing that trail of tears, the AURA astronomers said NASA should start investing now in the critical technologies needed to make future telescopes work.

So the High Definition telescope is not destined to be the next item on NASA's list, or even next to next. After Webb in the pipeline is the ungainly named Wfirst-Afta (don't ask) designed to investigate dark energy, the mysterious something that is speeding the expansion of the cosmos. That mission was the first priority of the 2010 survey, and it could lift off in 2024 if all goes well.

The High Definition Space Telescope stands at the end of an exciting line of exoplanet research. Thanks to the Kepler spacecraft, astronomers think they now know that roughly 10 percent of the stars in our galaxy have Earth-size planets at the so-called Goldilocks distance suitable for liquid water and life. But the planets Kepler has discovered are too far away — hundreds of light-years — to study closely.

There is already one rocket, the Delta IV Heavy, that could launch this telescope, and the Space Launch System that NASA is developing to send astronauts to deep space would be even better. Packed into a rocket, the telescope would unfold in space like a butterfly spreading its wings, a technique NASA hopes it has perfected with the Webb.

ELWOOD H. SMITH

Moreover, even a million miles from Earth, it could be service-able by robots or even astronauts. "It would be crazy not to do it," said Neil deGrasse Tyson, the director of the museum's Hayden Planetarium, who moderated a discussion of the telescope report. He noted that a million miles would be by far the farthest a human had ever been from Earth, smashing the record set when the Apollo 13 astronauts swung around the moon and reached a distance of 249,000 miles in 1970.

Standing in the back of the room at the museum was Michael Massimino, a former astronaut who twice worked on Hubble in orbit and is now a Columbia professor and adviser at the Intrepid Sea, Air & Space Museum. He said he would be happy to go. When I asked him afterward, he sadly agreed that by 2030, humans will still not have been any farther into space.

The biggest pending technical problem is suppressing the glare from stars to find their planets. The sun, for example, is 10 billion times brighter than the Earth. The future space telescope would be equipped with an internal coronagraph, a disk that blocks light from the central star, making a dim planet more visible, and perhaps eventually a star shade that would float miles out in front of it to do the same thing. Investing in this light-suppression technology now might prevent the cost overruns that led to the Webb telescope's nearly being canceled a few years ago.

Which raises the delicate issue of how much this would all cost.

Lacking the kind of detailed design from which estimates could be reliably made, Dr. Mountain and his colleagues said only that it would qualify as what NASA calls a "flagship mission," like Hubble. That puts it in the ballpark of $10 billion, the same as the cost of CERN's Large Hadron Collider, where the Higgs boson was discovered three years ago.

I used to think $10 billion was a lot of money before TARP, the Troubled Asset Relief Program, the $700 billion bailout that saved the banks in 2008 and apparently has brought happy days back to Wall Street. Compared with this, the science budget is chump change, lunch money at a place like Goldman Sachs. But if you think this is not a bargain, you need look only as far as your pocket. Companies like Google and Apple have leveraged modest investments in computer science in the 1960s into trillions of dollars of economic activity. Not even Arthur C. Clarke, the vaunted author and space-age prophet, saw that coming.

Which is to say that all that NASA money — whether for planetary probes or space station trips — is spent on Earth, on things that we like to say we want more of: high technology, education, a more skilled work force, jobs, pride in American and human innovation, not to mention greater cosmic awareness, a dose of perspective on our situation here among the stars.

Even if we never discover even a single microbe anywhere else, the money spent on the search for life out there will make life better for those of us stuck here on Earth.

There is nothing to be gained by delaying. As Dr. Seager from M.I.T. said, the central question — are we alone? — is not going away. "It will always have a price tag on it."

Speaking to the young people in the audience, Dr. Tyson said, "If you're 12 years old now, you'll be our age by the time it happens, and then you will be carrying the torch."

NASA Says Data Reveals an Earth-Like Planet, Kepler 452b

BY DENNIS OVERBYE | JULY 23, 2015

INCHING AHEAD on their quest for what they call Earth 2.0, astronomers from NASA's Kepler planet-hunting spacecraft announced on Thursday that they had found what might be one of the closest analogues to our own world yet.

It is a planet a little more than one and a half times as big in radius as Earth. Known as Kepler 452b, it circles a sunlike star in an orbit that takes 385 days, just slightly longer than our own year, putting it firmly in the "Goldilocks" habitable zone where the temperatures are lukewarm and suitable for liquid water on the surface — if it has a surface.

The new planet's size puts it right on the edge between being rocky like Earth and being a fluffy gas ball like Neptune, according to studies of other such exoplanets. In an email, Jon Jenkins of NASA's Ames Research Center, home of the Kepler project, and lead author of a paper being published in The Astronomical Journal, said the likelihood of the planet's being rocky was 50 percent to 62 percent, depending on uncertainties in the size of its home star. That would mean its mass is about five times that of Earth.

Such a planet would probably have a thick, cloudy atmosphere and active volcanoes, Dr. Jenkins said, and twice the gravity of Earth. Describing the planet during a news conference, Dr. Jenkins lapsed into lines from John Keats's poem "On First Looking Into Chapman's Homer": "Then felt I like some watcher of the skies / When a new planet swims into his ken."

The star that lights this planet's sky is about 1.5 billion years older than our sun and 20 percent more luminous, which has implications for the prospects of life, Dr. Jenkins said.

"We can think of Kepler-452b as an older, bigger cousin to Earth, providing an opportunity to understand and reflect upon Earth's evolving environment," he said. "It's awe-inspiring to consider that this planet has spent six billion years in the habitable zone of its star, longer than Earth. That's substantial opportunity for life to arise, should all the necessary ingredients and conditions for life exist on this planet."

Asked if any radio telescopes had pointed at the planet to try to detect extraterrestrial radio broadcasts, Dr. Jenkins said, "I hope so."

To determine whether Kepler 452b deserves a place on the honor roll of possible home worlds, however, astronomers have to measure its mass directly, which requires being close enough to observe the wobbling of its star as it is tugged around by the planet's gravity. For now, that is impossible, as Kepler 452b is 1,400 light-years away.

NASA AMES/JPL-CALTECH/T. PYLE

An artist's concept of Kepler 452b orbiting its star, 1,400 light-years from Earth. The planet's size puts it right on the edge between being rocky like Earth and a gas ball like Neptune.

The planet is the first to be confirmed in a new list of candidates unveiled by Kepler astronomers on Thursday. It brings the number of possible planets discovered by Kepler to 4,696, many of them small like Earth. "We are the bread crumbs of the universe," said Jeff Coughlin, of the SETI Institute in Mountain View, Calif., who compiled the catalog.

The spacecraft, launched in 2009, spent four years staring at a patch of the Milky Way on the border between the constellations Cygnus and Lyra, looking for the dips in starlight caused by the passage of planets. Its pointing system failed in 2013, but astronomers are still analyzing the data Kepler collected. Every time they sift through it, new planets pop out.

In the meantime, Kepler has switched to a different mode of observing in a mission called K2.

The NASA news conference coincided with a major anniversary: It was only 20 years ago this fall that Michel Mayor and Didier Queloz, of the University of Geneva, discovered a planet circling the star 51 Pegasi, about 50 light-years from here. It was the first planet known to belong to a sunlike star outside our solar system, and its discovery ignited an astronomical revolution.

Dr. Queloz, now at the University of Cambridge in England, said at the news conference, "This is a great time we live in."

"If we keep working so well and so enthusiastically," he went on, it is not too optimistic to think that in the future, "the issue of life on another planet will be solved."

Astronomers say they now know from Kepler that about 10 percent of the 200 billion stars in the Milky Way have potentially habitable Earth-size planets, Kepler 452b probably among them. This means that of the 600 stars within 30 light-years of Earth, there are roughly 60 E.T.-class abodes, planets that could be inspected by a future generation of telescopes.

Reaching for the Stars, Across 4.37 Light-Years

BY DENNIS OVERBYE | APRIL 12, 2016

CAN YOU FLY an iPhone to the stars?

In an attempt to leapfrog the planets and vault into the interstellar age, a bevy of scientists and other luminaries from Silicon Valley and beyond, led by Yuri Milner, a Russian philanthropist and Internet entrepreneur, announced a plan on Tuesday to send a fleet of robot spacecraft no bigger than iPhones to Alpha Centauri, the nearest star system, 4.37 light-years away.

If it all worked out — a cosmically big "if" that would occur decades and perhaps $10 billion from now — a rocket would deliver a "mother ship" carrying a thousand or so small probes to space. Once in orbit, the probes would unfold thin sails and then, propelled by powerful laser beams from Earth, set off one by one like a flock of migrating butterflies across the universe.

Within two minutes, the probes would be more than 600,000 miles from home — as far as the lasers could maintain a tight beam — and moving at a fifth of the speed of light. But it would still take 20 years for them to get to Alpha Centauri. Those that survived would zip past the star system, making measurements and beaming pictures back to Earth.

Much of this plan is probably half a lifetime away. Mr. Milner and his colleagues estimate that it could take 20 years to get the mission off the ground and into the heavens, 20 years to get to Alpha Centauri and another four years for the word from outer space to come home. And there is still the matter of attracting billions of dollars to pay for it.

"I think you and I will be happy to see the launch," Mr. Milner, 54, said in an interview, adding that progress in medicine and longevity would determine whether he would live to see the results.

"We came to the conclusion it can be done: interstellar travel," Mr. Milner said. He announced the project, called Breakthrough Starshot, in a news conference in New York on Tuesday, 55 years after Yuri Gagarin — for whom Mr. Milner is named — became the first human in space.

The English cosmologist and author Stephen Hawking is one of three members of the board of directors for the mission, along with Mr. Milner and Mark Zuckerberg, the Facebook founder.

"What makes human beings unique?" Dr. Hawking asked. He went on to say, "I believe that what makes us unique is transcending our limits."

Dr. Hawking added, "Today we commit to the next great leap in the cosmos, because we are human and our nature is to fly."

The project will be directed by Pete Worden, a former director of NASA's Ames Research Center. He has a prominent cast of advisers, including the Harvard astronomer Avi Loeb as chairman; the British

Yuri Milner, the internet entrepreneur and philanthropist, announces the Breakthrough Starshot initiative, at One World Trade Center in New York, April 12, 2016.

astronomer royal Martin Rees; the Nobel Prize-winning astronomer Saul Perlmutter, of the University of California, Berkeley; Ann Druyan, an executive producer of the television mini-series "Cosmos: A Spacetime Odyssey" and the widow of Carl Sagan; and the mathematician and author Freeman Dyson, of the Institute for Advanced Study in Princeton, N.J.

"There are about 20 key challenges we are asking the world's scientific experts to help us with — and we are willing to financially support their work," Dr. Worden said in an email.

A detailed technical description of the project appears on the project's website.

Estimating that the project could cost $5 billion to $10 billion, Mr. Milner is initially investing $100 million for research and development. He said he was hoping to lure other investors, especially from international sources. Both NASA and the European Space Agency have been briefed on the project, Dr. Worden said.

Most of that money would go toward a giant laser array, which could be used to repeatedly send probes toward any star (as long as the senders were not looking for return mail anytime soon) or around the solar system, perhaps to fly through the ice plumes of Saturn's moon Enceladus, which might contain microbes — tiny forms of life.

In a sense, the start of this space project reflects the make-it-or-break-it mode of Silicon Valley. Rather than send one big, expensive spacecraft on a journey of years, send thousands of cheap ones. If some break or collide with space junk, others can take their place.

Interstellar travel is a daunting and humbling notion, but Alpha Centauri is an alluring target for such a trip: It is the closest star system to our own, and there might be planets in the system. The system, which looks to the naked eye like one star, consists of three: Alpha Centauri A and Alpha Centauri B, which circle each other, and Proxima Centauri, which may be circling the other two. In recent years, astronomers have amassed data suggesting the possibility of an Earth-size planet orbiting Alpha Centauri B.

It would take Voyager 1, humanity's most distant space probe, more than 70,000 years to reach Alpha Centauri if it were headed in that direction, which it is not.

Over the years, a variety of propulsion plans have been hatched to cross the void more quickly. In 1962, shortly after lasers were invented, Robert Forward, a physicist and science fiction author, suggested they could be used to push sails in space.

In 2011, Darpa, the Defense Advanced Research Projects Agency, got into the act with 100 Year Starship, a contest to develop a business plan for interstellar travel.

By all accounts, Mr. Milner was initially skeptical of an interstellar probe. But three trends seemingly unrelated to space travel — advances in nanotechnology and lasers and the relentless march of Moore's Law, making circuits ever smaller and more powerful — have converged in what he called "a surprising way."

It is now possible to fit the entire probe with computers, cameras and electrical power, a package with a mass of only one gram, a thirtieth of an ounce.

That, Dr. Loeb said, is about what the guts of an iPhone, stripped of its packaging and displays, amount to.

Power would come from a tiny radioactive source like americium, the element in smoke detectors. Propulsion would come from foil sails that would unfold to catch laser light.

The laser is the most intimidating and expensive of the challenges. It would have to generate 100 gigawatts of power for the two minutes needed to accelerate the butterfly probes to a fifth of the speed of light (subjecting its tiny innards to 60,000 times the force of normal gravity, by the way). That is about as much energy as it takes for a space shuttle to lift off, Dr. Loeb said, and about 100 times the output of a typical nuclear power plant.

To achieve that energy would require an array about a mile across combining thousands of lasers firing in perfect unison.

Moreover, to keep the beam tightly focused on one probe at a time would require an adaptive optics system that compensated for atmospheric turbulence — something astronomers know how to do over a span of 10 meters, the size of a big telescope mirror now, but not over a mile.

Posing another challenge is the design of the sails, which would have to be very thin and able to reflect the laser light without absorbing any of its energy. Absorbing as little as one part in 100,000 of the laser energy would vaporize the sail.

Another challenge might simply be to the imagination. Nobody knows what the Starshot fleet might find out.

"Looking is very different from going and visiting," Dr. Loeb said.

As he noted, referring to recent physics experiments, "Nature teaches us that its imagination is better than ours."

Yes, There Have Been Aliens

OPINION | BY ADAM FRANK | JUNE 10, 2016

LAST MONTH astronomers from the Kepler spacecraft team announced the discovery of 1,284 new planets, all orbiting stars outside our solar system. The total number of such "exoplanets" confirmed via Kepler and other methods now stands at more than 3,000.

This represents a revolution in planetary knowledge. A decade or so ago the discovery of even a single new exoplanet was big news. Not anymore. Improvements in astronomical observation technology have moved us from retail to wholesale planet discovery. We now know, for example, that every star in the sky likely hosts at least one planet.

But planets are only the beginning of the story. What everyone wants to know is whether any of these worlds has aliens living on it. Does our newfound knowledge of planets bring us any closer to answering that question?

A little bit, actually, yes. In a paper published in the May issue of the journal Astrobiology, the astronomer Woodruff Sullivan and I show that while we do not know if any advanced extraterrestrial civilizations currently exist in our galaxy, we now have enough information to conclude that they almost certainly existed at some point in cosmic history.

Among scientists, the probability of the existence of an alien society with which we might make contact is discussed in terms of something called the Drake equation. In 1961, the National Academy of Sciences asked the astronomer Frank Drake to host a scientific meeting on the possibilities of "interstellar communication." Since the odds of contact with alien life depended on how many advanced extraterrestrial civilizations existed in the galaxy, Drake identified seven factors on which that number would depend, and incorporated them into an equation.

The first factor was the number of stars born each year. The second was the fraction of stars that had planets. After that came the number of planets per star that traveled in orbits in the right locations for life to form (assuming life requires liquid water). The next factor was the fraction of such planets where life actually got started. Then came factors for the fraction of life-bearing planets on which intelligence and advanced civilizations (meaning radio signal-emitting) evolved. The final factor was the average lifetime of a technological civilization.

Drake's equation was not like Einstein's E=mc2. It was not a statement of a universal law. It was a mechanism for fostering organized discussion, a way of understanding what we needed to know to answer the question about alien civilizations. In 1961, only the first factor — the number of stars born each year — was understood. And that level of ignorance remained until very recently.

That's why discussions of extraterrestrial civilizations, no matter how learned, have historically boiled down to mere expressions of hope or pessimism. What, for example, is the fraction of planets that form life? Optimists might marshal sophisticated molecular biological models to argue for a large fraction. Pessimists then cite their own scientific data to argue for a fraction closer to 0. But with only one example of a life-bearing planet (ours), it's hard to know who is right.

Or consider the average lifetime of a civilization. Humans have been using radio technology for only about 100 years. How much longer will our civilization last? A thousand more years? A hundred thousand more? Ten million more? If the average lifetime for a civilization is short, the galaxy is likely to be unpopulated most of the time. Once again, however, with only one example to draw from, it's back to a battle between pessimists and optimists.

But our new planetary knowledge has removed some of the uncertainty from this debate. Three of the seven terms in Drake's equation are now known. We know the number of stars born each year. We know that the percentage of stars hosting planets is about 100. And we also know that about 20 to 25 percent of those planets are in the right place for life to form. This puts us in a position, for the first time, to say something definitive about extraterrestrial civilizations — if we ask the right question.

GÉRARD DUBOIS

In our recent paper, Professor Sullivan and I did this by shifting the focus of Drake's equation. Instead of asking how many civilizations currently exist, we asked what the probability is that ours is the only technological civilization that has ever appeared. By asking this question, we could bypass the factor about the average lifetime of a civilization. This left us with only three unknown factors, which we combined into one "biotechnical" probability: the likelihood of the creation of life, intelligent life and technological capacity.

You might assume this probability is low, and thus the chances remain small that another technological civilization arose. But what our calculation revealed is that even if this probability is assumed to be extremely low, the odds that we are not the first technological civilization are actually high. Specifically, unless the probability for evolving a civilization on a habitable-zone planet is less than one in 10 billion trillion, then we are not the first.

To give some context for that figure: In previous discussions of the Drake equation, a probability for civilizations to form of one in 10 billion per planet was considered highly pessimistic. According to our finding, even if you grant that level of pessimism, a trillion civilizations still would have appeared over the course of cosmic history.

In other words, given what we now know about the number and orbital positions of the galaxy's planets, the degree of pessimism required to doubt the existence, at some point in time, of an advanced extraterrestrial civilization borders on the irrational.

In science an important step forward can be finding a question that can be answered with the data at hand. Our paper did just this. As for the big question — whether any other civilizations currently exist — we may have to wait a long while for relevant data. But we should not underestimate how far we have come in a short time.

ADAM FRANK is an astrophysics professor at the University of Rochester, a co-founder of NPR's 13.7 Cosmos and Culture blog and the author of "About Time: Cosmology and Culture at the Twilight of the Big Bang."

What's So Special About Another Earth?

OPINION | BY LISA MESSERI | AUG. 25, 2016

CHARLOTTESVILLE, VA. — Yesterday, the European Southern Observatory announced that astronomers have detected a planet the size of Earth orbiting our nearest star, Proxima Centauri. We discover hundreds of "exoplanets" every year, but this one is different: It orbits its star at just the right distance so that, in theory, it's possible it could sustain life. This detection of a "goldilocks" planet so close to our own marks a significant achievement for exoplanet astronomy, the young field devoted to the search for and study of planets orbiting stars other than our sun.

The European Southern Observatory's news release explains that Proxima Centauri, unlike the other two stars in its system, is a red dwarf, smaller and cooler than our sun. Although liquid water, that all-important life sustaining substance, might exist on the surface of this planet, its 11-day orbit and strong radiation would create a climate very different from Earth's. Standing on the surface, one would see not the familiar blue sky; more likely, it would be an alien red.

The astronomers are of course well aware of these dissimilarities. Why, then, do they still insist on categorizing this planet as Earth-like? Some fantasize that "another earth" could be a celestial refuge if we end up destroying our own. Another answer is that detecting a planet like ours capable of hosting life brings us one step closer to answering the ultimate question of whether or not we are alone in the universe — the end of our "cosmic loneliness," as the science reporter Dennis Overbye wrote in this paper.

But today's announcement will not readily lead to contact with an intelligent alien. This discovery, more than offering a connection between life-forms, is much more about us connecting with what Earth is, as a place and as our home.

Exoplanet astronomy flourished with the 2009 launch of Kepler, a space telescope dedicated to finding exoplanets. At the time, I was a graduate student at MIT studying the anthropology and history of science, in particular the men and women studying planets as close as Mars and as distant as the exoplanets Kepler was rapidly finding. What drove them? Exoplanets are rather insignificant astronomical objects, but I learned how these scientists transformed planets into places and in so doing have populated the cosmos with hundreds of meaningful worlds.

In this community, the ideal is the Earthlike exoplanet. As an exoplanet graduate student once told me, "In the end, we want to find other Earths. We want to find something similar to us."

In 2008, a group of astronomers reflected on the philosophical implications of such a discovery, writing that it would tempt us "with wild dreams of flight," and we would "refocus our energies to hasten the day when our descendants might dare to try to bridge the gulf between two inhabited worlds." The cover of the current issue of New Scientist offers a beautiful, welcoming artist's rendering of the newly discovered planet orbiting Proxima Centauri. "We've found an Earthlike planet around our nearest star," the cover asks. "Should we go there?"

Dreams of interstellar journeys or contacting alien life overshadow a less sensational but equally meaningful aspect of this discovery: Amid all of the fantastical configurations in the universe, we most desire to connect with a rather unremarkable ball of rock, ice and gas, for the simple but powerful reason that it reminds us of our home. To even claim the existence of an Earthlike planet is also to claim, rightly or wrongly, that we know and understand our planet. Despite a changing climate and an unsettled population, there is some essence of our planet that we can recognize and point to, saying, "that is us."

When I spoke with astronomers about methods for detecting Earth's twin, I was struck that what they were searching for was Earth at its most pristine. One reason the search for an Earthlike planet is so compelling is that it is unexpectedly nostalgic. It propagates an imagination of Earth as an ideal, edenic home. This is a planetary home simpler than the one we grapple with on a daily basis; a home that we might fantasize was the planet of our youth.

Describing how exoplanet astronomy connects us to our past, an astronomer described for me why her field matters. "People always want to know where we came from, where we really came from," she said. "Other planets are a big part of answering that question."

As they say, you can't go home again. The discovery of the exoplanet orbiting Proxima Centauri will be closely studied in the coming years. I suspect we'll find a fascinating world, if starkly different from Earth. That doesn't make the discovery any less exciting or important. But it does remind us that Earth is special. As we peer deeper and with greater acuity into the universe, we are simultaneously forced to appreciate the complexity of all worlds, including our own.

LISA MESSERI (@lmesseri), an assistant professor of science, technology and society at the University of Virginia, is the author of "Placing Outer Space: An Earthly Ethnography of Other Worlds."

7 Earth-Size Planets Orbit Dwarf Star, NASA and European Astronomers Say

BY KENNETH CHANG | FEB. 22, 2017

NOT JUST ONE, but seven Earth-size planets that could potentially harbor life have been identified orbiting a tiny star not too far away, offering the first realistic opportunity to search for signs of alien life outside the solar system.

The planets orbit a dwarf star named Trappist-1, about 40 light-years, or 235 trillion miles, from Earth. That is quite close in cosmic terms, and by happy accident, the orientation of the orbits of the seven planets allows them to be studied in great detail.

One or more of the exoplanets in this new system could be at the right temperature to be awash in oceans of water, astronomers said, based on the distance of the planets from the dwarf star.

"This is the first time so many planets of this kind are found around the same star," Michael Gillon, an astronomer at the University of Liege in Belgium and the leader of an international team that has been observing Trappist-1, said during a telephone news conference organized by the journal Nature, which published the findings on Wednesday.

Scientists could even discover compelling evidence of aliens.

"I think that we have made a crucial step toward finding if there is life out there," said Amaury H. M. J. Triaud, an astronomer at the University of Cambridge in England and another member of the research team. "Here, if life managed to thrive and releases gases similar to that we have on Earth, then we will know."

Cool red dwarfs are the most common type of star, so astronomers are likely to find more planetary systems like that around Trappist-1 in the coming years.

"You can just imagine how many worlds are out there that have a shot to becoming a habitable ecosystem," Thomas Zurbuchen, associate administrator of NASA's science mission directorate, said during a

NASA news conference on Wednesday. "Are we alone out there? We're making a step forward with this — a leap forward, in fact — towards answering that question."

Telescopes on the ground now and the Hubble Space Telescope in orbit will be able to discern some of the molecules in the planetary atmospheres. The James Webb Space Telescope, scheduled to launch next year, will peer at the infrared wavelengths of light, ideal for studying Trappist-1.

Comparisons among the different conditions of the seven will also be revealing.

"The Trappist-1 planets make the search for life in the galaxy imminent," said Sara Seager, an astronomer at the Massachusetts Institute of Technology who was not a member of the research team. "For the first time ever, we don't have to speculate. We just have to wait and then make very careful observations and see what is in the atmospheres of the Trappist planets."

Even if the planets all turn out to be lifeless, scientists will have learned more about what keeps life from flourishing.

Astronomers always knew other stars must have planets, but until a couple of decades ago, they had not been able to spot them. Now they have confirmed more than 3,400, according to the Open Exoplanet Catalog. (An exoplanet is a planet around a star other than the sun.)

The authors of the Nature paper include Didier Queloz, one of the astronomers who discovered in 1995 the first known exoplanet around a sunlike star.

While the Trappist planets are about the size of Earth — give or take 25 percent in diameter — the star is very different from our sun.

Trappist-1, named after a robotic telescope in the Atacama Desert of Chile that the astronomers initially used to study the star, is what astronomers call an "ultracool dwarf," with only one-twelfth the mass of the sun and a surface temperature of 4,150 degrees Fahrenheit, much cooler than the 10,000 degrees radiating from the sun. Trappist is a shortening of Transiting Planets and Planetesimals Small Telescope.

During the NASA news conference, Dr. Gillon gave a simple analogy: If our sun were the size of a basketball, Trappist-1 would be a golf ball.

Until the last few years, scientists looking for life elsewhere in the galaxy have focused on finding Earth-size planets around sun-like stars. But it is hard to pick out the light of a planet from the glare of a bright star. Small dim dwarfs are much easier to study.

Last year, astronomers announced the discovery of an Earth-size planet around Proxima Centauri, the closest star at 4.24 light-years away. That discovery was made using a different technique that does not allow for study of the atmosphere.

Trappist-1 periodically dimmed noticeably, indicating that a planet might be passing in front of the star, blocking part of the light. From the shape of the dips, the astronomers calculate the size of the planet.

Trappist-1's light dipped so many times that the astronomers concluded, in research reported last year, that there were at least three planets around the star. Telescopes from around the world then also observed Trappist-1, as did the Spitzer Space Telescope of NASA.

Spitzer observed Trappist-1 nearly around the clock for 20 days, capturing 34 transits. Together with the ground observations, it let the scientists calculate not three planets, but seven. The planets are too small and too close to the star to be photographed directly.

All seven are very close to the dwarf star, circling more quickly than the planets in our solar system. The innermost completes an orbit in just 1.5 days. The farthest one completes an orbit in about 20 days. That makes the planetary system more like the moons of Jupiter than a larger planetary system like our solar system.

"They form a very compact system," Dr. Gillon said, "the planets being pulled close to each other and very close to the star."

In addition, the orbital periods of the inner six suggest that the planets formed farther away from the star and then were all gradually pulled inward, Dr. Gillon said.

Because the planets are so close to a cool star, their surfaces could be at the right temperatures to have water flow, considered one of the essential ingredients for life.

The fourth, fifth and sixth planets orbit in the star's "habitable zone," where the planets could sport oceans. So far that is just speculation, but by measuring which wavelengths of light are blocked by the planet, scientists will be able to figure out what gases float in the atmospheres of the seven planets.

So far, they have confirmed for the two innermost planets that they are not enveloped in hydrogen. That means they are rocky like Earth, ruling out the possibility that they were mini-Neptune gas planets that are prevalent around many other stars.

Because the planets are so close to Trappist-1, they have quite likely become "gravitationally locked" to the star, always with one side of the planets facing the star, much as it is always the same side of Earth's moon facing Earth. That would mean one side would be warmer, but an atmosphere would distribute heat, and the scientists said that would not be an insurmountable obstacle for life.

For a person standing on one of the planets, it would be a dim environment, with perhaps only about one two-hundredth the light that we see from the sun on Earth, Dr. Triaud said. (That would still be brighter than the moon at night.) The star would be far bigger. On Trappist-1f, the fifth planet, the star would be three times as wide as the sun seen from Earth.

As for the color of the star, "we had a debate about that," Dr. Triaud said.

Some of the scientists expected a deep red, but with most of the star's light emitted at infrared wavelengths and out of view of human eyes, perhaps a person would "see something more salmon-y," Dr. Triaud said.

NASA released a poster illustrating what the sky of the fourth planet might look like.

If observations reveal oxygen in a planet's atmosphere, that could point to photosynthesis of plants — although not conclusively. But oxygen together with methane, ozone and carbon dioxide, particularly in certain proportions, "would tell us that there is life with 99 percent confidence," Dr. Gillon said.

Astronomers expect that a few decades of technological advances are needed before similar observations can be made of Earthlike planets around larger, brighter sunlike stars.

Dr. Triaud said that if there is life around Trappist-1, "then it's good we didn't wait too long."

"If there isn't, then we have learned something quite deep about where life can emerge," he continued.

The discovery might also mean that scientists who have been searching for radio signals from alien civilizations might also have been searching in the wrong places if most habitable planets orbit dwarfs, which live far longer than larger stars like the sun.

The SETI Institute in Mountain View, Calif., is using the Allen Telescope Array, a group of 42 radio dishes in California, to scrutinize 20,000 red dwarfs. "This result is kind of a justification for that project," said Seth Shostak, an astronomer at the institute.

"If you're looking for complex biology — intelligent aliens that might take a long time to evolve from pond scum — older could be better," Dr. Shostak said. "It seems a good bet that the majority of clever beings populating the universe look up to see a dim, reddish sun hanging in their sky. And at least they wouldn't have to worry about sun block."

Earth-Size Planets Among Final Tally of NASA's Kepler Telescope

BY DENNIS OVERBYE | JUNE 19, 2017

MOUNTAIN VIEW, CALIF. — Are we still alone?

Setting the stage for the next chapter in the quest to end cosmic loneliness, astronomers released a list on Monday of 4,034 objects they are 90 percent sure are planets orbiting other stars.

The new list is the final and most reliable result of a four-year cosmic census of a tiny region of the Milky Way by NASA's Kepler spacecraft.

"The search for planets is the search for life," said Natalie Batalha, a Kepler mission scientist from NASA's Ames Research Center. "These results will form the basis for future searches for life."

Extrapolated from one small patch to the entire sky, the data will help NASA design a space telescope for the 2030s or thereabouts, big and powerful enough to discern the images of planets around other stars.

The catalog — the eighth in the endeavor — was released at a meeting of exoplanet astronomers here at the Ames Research Center that represents a last hurrah for the survey mission, which will end on Sept. 30. The space telescope itself is doing fine, and it has embarked on a new program of short-term searches called K2.

Among other things, Dr. Batalha said, for the first time there is at least one planet, known as KOI 7711 (for Kepler Object of Interest), that almost matches the Earth, at only 30 percent wider and with an orbit of almost exactly one year.

In all, there are 219 new planet candidates in the catalog. Ten of them, moreover, are in the habitable zones of their stars, the so-called Goldilocks realm, where the heat from their stars is neither too cold nor too hot for liquid water.

They are fascinating, but Kepler's mission is not to pinpoint the next tourist destination — it is to find out on average how far away such places are. Or, as Dr. Batalha said, "We're not stamp collecting, we're doing statistics."

Another result reported on Monday deepened a mystery about how nature goes about making planets. Over the years, Kepler has discovered that nature likes to make small planets, but it makes them in two ways: rocky, like Earth, and gaseous, like Neptune.

A new study, led by Benjamin Fulton of the California Institute of Technology, of 1,305 stars and 2,025 planets that orbit them has found a curious gap in the planet population that seems to mark the boundary between rocky planets, which can be up to one and a half times the size of the Earth, (sometimes called super-Earths) and gaseous planets, so-called mini-Neptunes, which are more than about twice the size of Earth. (Neptune itself is four times the diameter and 17 times the mass of Earth.)

Andrew Howard, a Caltech professor who worked with Mr. Fulton, compared this splitting of small planets into two populations to discovering a major branch point in the tree of life.

All planets seem to start out with about the same amount of rock in their cores, he said. How much gas — mostly hydrogen and helium from the primordial cloud that birthed us — adheres to them makes all the difference. While the Earth, which has hardly any atmosphere at all by weight, is a pleasant place, the pressure on a world with just a little more gas would be toxic.

"It doesn't take much gas to puff up a planet," Mr. Fulton said. "This has significance in the search for life."

Presumably, Mr. Fulton said, the planets that are rocky now, like Earth, had their gassy envelopes stripped away or evaporated by radiation from their stars. But nobody really knows how it works. Adding to the mystery is that our own solar system has no example of a mini-Neptune, and yet they are prevalent in alien planet systems.

In 1984, William Borucki, a NASA physicist and expert on photometry, or measuring light intensity, and a colleague, the late David Koch, had a pretty simple idea: If a distant star blinked or dimmed periodically, it might mean there was a planet going around it. All you had to do was watch, very precisely and steadily.

At the time, nobody knew if any other stars besides the sun harbored planets. NASA turned down Mr. Borucki and Dr. Koch five times before the experiment was finally approved in 2001.

Kepler was launched into an orbit around the sun on March 6, 2009, with a simple mission: to stare at some 160,000 stars in a patch of sky in the constellation Cygnus. If any of those stars dimmed periodically, the size of the dip in light could tell you how big the planet passing in front of it was. The length of time between blinks would tell you how many days long its year was.

In the case of the Earth as seen from space, the amount of dimmed light would be about 0.008 percent of the sun's light — about as much as a few fleas crossing a car headlight — once a year. Kepler can detect the equivalent of one flea in the headlight. Since the rules of engagement required three transits to verify a planet, that meant it would take that many years on average to discover an exact analog of our own home: Earth 2.0, it was sometimes called.

At the time Kepler was launched, more than 300 exoplanets, planets outside our solar system, had been found, mostly by examining stars one by one to see if they showed signs of being perturbed — "wobbled" — by the gravitational pull of a planet or planets.

Those on the Kepler team did not know what they were going to find. Dr. Batalha recalled that they had argued about how to construct their catalog of interesting objects — whether it would only be able to go to 1,000 or 10,000. In the end, they almost ran out of room on the list, Dr. Batalha recalled, which wound up running to 9,000.

In its first few months of observations, Kepler almost immediately doubled the number of known or suspected exoplanets. The tally kept climbing, to 1,200 by February 2011 and to more than 4,700 a year ago.

Unfortunately, Kepler also discovered that stars are more jittery than astronomers had expected, complicating the problem of

An artist's conception of KOI-961, a star system detected by the Kepler space telescope. It has three of the smallest planets known so far to orbit a star other than our sun.

discerning planet transits from random fluctuations in the stars. This volatility, or noise, made it especially hard for Kepler's crew members to see what they most wanted to see — small rocky planets with years as long as the Earth's.

Citing this interference, Dr. Batalha and her team received an extension of Kepler's original mission in 2013, but shortly thereafter one of the reaction wheels that kept the spacecraft pointed failed, ending its ability to keep staring at the same 160,000 stars.

"We had to live with what we got," Dr. Batalha said.

The final catalog, compiled by Susan Thompson of the SETI Institute, is slightly smaller than the list from a year ago, thanks to a new algorithm known as Robovetter that automatically corrects the Kepler data for the effects of the extra noise. The result is guaranteed to be 90 percent accurate.

"With this catalog, we are turning from individual planets to trying to understand the demographics of these worlds, which are similar to Earth," Dr. Thompson said.

About four years ago, Erik Petigura, now at Caltech, extrapolated boldly from the Kepler data and estimated that about a fifth of the sun-like stars in the galaxy had habitable planets. About one in four of the smaller stars, known as red dwarfs, also harbor rocky habitable-zone planets, said Courtney Dressing, an astronomer at Caltech.

The data suggested that there could be billions of Earth-size planets in the Milky Way basking in lukewarm conditions suitable for liquid water, and so perhaps life as we think we know it.

The Kepler team will refine those estimates with their new data.

In the meantime the baton is being passed to a new satellite, TESS, for Transiting Exoplanet Survey Satellite, led by George Ricker of M.I.T., to be launched next year. It will use the same technique as Kepler to look at broad areas of the sky, searching for planets around the brightest and nearest stars.

The James Webb Space Telescope, which can be used to investigate the atmospheres of some of these planets, will also be launched next year.

"These missions will help us answer questions mankind has asked since the dawn of civilization," Mr. Borucki said. "Where did we come from? Are we alone?"

Meet TESS, Seeker of Alien Worlds

BY DENNIS OVERBYE | MARCH 26, 2018

NASA's new spacecraft, to be launched next month, will give scientists a much clearer view of the planets orbiting stars near to us.

KENNEDY SPACE CENTER, FLA. — The search for cosmic real estate is about to begin anew.

No earlier than 6:32 p.m. on April 16, in NASA's fractured parlance, a little spacecraft known as the Transiting Exoplanet Survey Satellite, or TESS, bristling with cameras and ambition, will ascend on a SpaceX Falcon 9 rocket in a blaze of smoke and fire and take up a lengthy residence between the moon and the Earth.

There it will spend the next two years, at least, scanning the sky for alien worlds.

TESS is the latest effort to try to answer questions that have intrigued humans for millenniums and dominated astronomy for the last three decades: Are we alone? Are there other Earths? Evidence of even a single microbe anywhere else in the galaxy would rock science.

Not so long ago, astronomers didn't know if there were planets outside our solar system or, if there were, whether they could ever be found. But starting with the 1995 discovery of a planet circling the sun-like star 51 Pegasi, there has been a revolution.

NASA's Kepler spacecraft, launched in 2009, discovered some 4,000 possible planets in one small patch of the Milky Way near the constellation Cygnus. Kepler went on to survey other star fields only briefly after its pointing system broke. After nine years in space, it's running out of fuel.

Thanks to efforts like Kepler's, astronomers now think there are billions of potentially habitable planets in our galaxy, which means the nearest one could be as close as 10 to 15 light-years from here.

And so the torch is passed. It's now TESS's job to find those nearby planets, the ones close enough to scrutinize with telescopes, or even for an interstellar robot to visit.

"Most of the stars with planets are far away," said Sara Seager, a planetary scientist at the Massachusetts Institute of Technology and a member of the TESS team, referring to Kepler's bounty. "TESS will fill in planets around nearby stars."

George Ricker, an M.I.T. researcher and the leader of the TESS team, expects to find some 500 Earth-sized planets within 300 light-years of here, close enough for a coming generation of telescopes on the ground and in space to examine for habitability — or perhaps even inhabitants.

But there will be more than planets in the universe, according to TESS.

"TESS is going to be a lot of fun," Dr. Ricker said. "There are 20 million stars we can look at." The spacecraft will be able to do precise brightness measurements of every glint in the heavens, he said. "Galaxies, stars, active galactic nuclei," his voice trailing off.

Most of the exoplanets will be orbiting stars called red dwarfs, much smaller and cooler than the sun. They make up the vast majority of stars in our neighborhood (and in the universe) and presumably lay claim to most of the planets.

Like Kepler, TESS will hunt those planets by monitoring the light from stars and detecting slight dips, momentary fading indicating that a planet has passed in front of its star.

The mission's planners say they eventually expect to catalog 20,000 new exoplanet candidates of all shapes and sizes. In particular, they have promised to come up with the masses and orbits of 50 new planets that are less than four times the size of the Earth.

Most of the planets in the universe are in this range — between the sizes of Earth and Neptune. But since there are no examples of them in our own solar system, as Dr. Seager notes, "we don't know anything about them."

Are they so-called "superearths," mostly rock with a veil of atmosphere, or "mini-Neptunes" with small cores buried deep inside extensive balls of gas?

Data from Kepler and astronomers suggests that the difference is mass: fertile rocks often are less than one and a half times the size of the Earth, while barren ice clouds often are bigger. Where the line really is, and how many planets fall on one side or the other, could determine how many worlds out there are balls of freezing vapor or potential gardens.

"We need to make precise mass measurements," said David Latham of the Harvard-Smithsonian Center for Astrophysics, who is in charge of organizing astronomers to follow up the TESS observations.

To that end, the team has procured 80 nights of observing time a year for the next five years on a spectrograph called Harps North, which resides on an Italian telescope on the island of La Palma in the Canary Islands, a part of Spain off the coast of Africa.

Harps — for High Accuracy Radial velocity Planet Searcher — can measure the mass of a planet by how much it makes its home star wobble as it goes around in an orbit. Such measurements, if precise enough could help distinguish the composition and structure of these bodies.

TESS is one of NASA's smaller missions, with a budget of $200 million; by comparison, Kepler had a budget of about $650 million.

Recently TESS, partly clad in shiny aluminum foil, stubby solar panels folded modestly against its side, was sitting on a round pedestal inside a plastic tent. The tent occupied one corner of a cavernous "clean room" in a remote building on the scrubby outskirts of the space center here, amid palms and canals and flocks of cormorants.

The spacecraft is about the size of a bulky, oddly shaped refrigerator, festooned not with magnets but with mysterious nozzles and connectors. Four pairs of blue-clad legs were sticking out from underneath the pedestal, as if high-tech mechanics were working under a car.

The engineers were taping plaques to the bottom of the spacecraft, including a memory chip containing drawings by schoolchildren who had been asked to imagine exoplanets might look like.

Standing to the side, in a "bunny suit" of protective material that left only his bespectacled eyes visible, Dr. Ricker was staring into the tent at his new spacecraft, as if he were watching his car get fixed, and exchanging rocket talk with the engineers who had designed and built it.

Dr. Ricker has been a rocket scientist, building astronomical satellites to be shot into space, for pretty much his entire career as a researcher at M.I.T.'s Kavli Institute for Astrophysics and Space Research.

Most of his previous projects involved measuring X-rays or gamma rays from various snaps, crackles and pops in the cosmos, most recently the High Energy Transient Explorer, used to study the cataclysms known as gamma-ray bursts.

Asked if planets represented a departure for him, Dr. Ricker shrugged, "Not so much." All his work has involved delicate measurements of things changing, what he called "time-domain astronomy."

The key to this work is to maintain very stable and sensitive detectors — the imaging chips that are elite relatives of the sensors in your smartphone — so that they can reliably record the changes in brightness, just a few parts per million, that signal a planet passing by its star.

Dr. Ricker said he and his colleagues had started "noodling" about a planet-finding mission back in 2006. After they lost out in a competition for NASA's Small Explorers program, which are less expensive missions, the scientists re-entered a competition for a larger mission in 2010 — and won.

They had gone to great lengths to design a compact spacecraft that would fit the rockets NASA used for Small Explorers, and so were nonplused when NASA selected SpaceX's Falcon 9, which can carry a much larger payload, to launch the TESS mission.

This is the first time NASA has purchased a ride from SpaceX, the rocket company run by Elon Musk, for one of its science missions. All eyes will be on the launchpad, given SpaceX's history of occasionally providing unhappy, if spectacular, denouements to missions.

A report released this month by NASA showed that the space agency and SpaceX still disagree on what exactly went wrong two-

and-a half years ago when a mission to resupply the International Space Station disintegrated in flight. In a second mishap in 2016, a Falcon 9 blew up during a launchpad test, destroying a communications satellite whose customers included Facebook.

Unbowed, SpaceX and its founder Mr. Musk have plowed on, with 22 consecutive launches of its Falcon and a maiden flight in February for the Falcon Heavy, the world's most powerful rocket, which shot one of Mr. Musk's Tesla convertibles past Mars into orbit around the sun.

"TESS looks like a little toy inside the Falcon 9," Dr. Ricker said. But a toy with potential.

On top of the spacecraft are four small cameras, each with a 24-degree field of view, a stretch of sky about the size of the Orion constellation.

The cameras will stare at adjacent sections of sky for 27 days at a time, and then step to the next spot. In the course of the first year, the researchers will survey the entire southern hemisphere of the sky; in the second year, they will stitch together the northern sky. If the mission is extended beyond two years, they will repeat.

Dr. Ricker and his colleagues have prepared a list of 200,000 nearby stars whose brightness will be measured and reported every two minutes in what they call the spacecraft's "postage stamp" mode. Meanwhile, images of the entire 24-degree swaths of sky will be recorded every half-hour.

That cadence is perfect for finding and studying current favorites in the race to locate habitable exoplanets, namely those circling the ubiquitous red dwarf stars, or M dwarfs, in astronomical jargon. "This is the era of the M dwarf," Dr. Seager said.

Because they are so much cooler and less luminous than the sun, their "Goldilocks" zones — where in principle liquid water is possible — lie only a few million miles out from each star, instead of the 90 million miles from which the Earth circles the sun.

At the shorter distance, a year in the life of a red dwarf planet is only 10 to 30 days. If TESS is watching that bit of the sky for 27 days straight, it may see three dips in brightness because of transits, enough to certify the planet as a real candidate and to start investigating its reality.

But reality, as Dr. Seager noted, might not be the same as habitability, at least for the fragile likes of us. Red dwarfs are very unstable and given to violent solar flares, she said.

Analyzing data from an 80-day Kepler observation of the Trappist system, involving at least seven Earth-sized planets tightly packed around a star about 40 light-years from here, Hungarian astronomers counted 42 solar flares raining lethal radiation through the little planetary system.

At least one, Dr. Seager pointed out, was as energetic as a famous solar flare called the Carrington Event in 1859, which destroyed telegraph service on Earth and sent auroras as far south as the Equator.

"Personally, I will always hold out for the true Earth twin, one we feel a kinship with," Dr. Seager said, referring to a planet like ours that circles a bigger star like the sun.

To start its excellent adventure, TESS will be launched into an unusually eccentric orbit that takes the satellite all the way out to the moon at its farthest point. Gravitational interaction with the moon will then keep TESS in a stable 13.7-day orbit for as long as 1,000 years, Dr. Ricker said.

The great apogee, the farthest distance from Earth, will minimize obstruction and interference from our planet. The spacecraft will radio its data back once every orbit, when it is closest to Earth, at about 67,000 miles up.

Dr. Latham called it "a slick orbit." But it will take almost two months and many rocket burns to get there and begin to do science. If all goes well, that would be the middle of June.

Sometime during that process, Dr. Ricker said, the team will turn the spacecraft's cameras on the Earth for a last look at home.

Asked if he was ready to be Mr. Exoplanet, Dr. Ricker winced. "What I'm looking forward to," he said, "is getting some data to look at."

CHAPTER 2

National Space Programs Evolve and Compete

In 2011, the NASA space shuttle program came to an end, diminishing American dominance of human spaceflight. Nations like China, India and Japan joined existing space powers like Russia and the European Union, using ambitious space programs to bolster international prestige. NASA, despite frequent changes in priorities from president to president, has continued to contribute to space research with major development projects such as the Kepler Space Telescope, in operation since 2009, and the James Webb Space Telescope, due to launch in 2021.

For NASA, Longest Countdown Awaits

BY KENNETH CHANG | JAN. 24, 2011

WHERE TO NEXT? And when?

For NASA, as it attempts to squeeze a workable human spaceflight program into a tight federal budget, the answers appear to be "somewhere" and "not anytime soon."

When the space shuttles are retired this year — and only one flight remains for each of the three — NASA will no longer have its own means for getting American astronauts to space.

What comes next is a muddle.

The program to send astronauts back to the moon, known as Constellation, was canceled last year.

In its place, Congress has asked NASA to build a heavy-lift rocket, one that can go deep into space carrying big loads. But NASA says it cannot possibly build such a rocket with the budget and schedule it has been given.

Another crucial component of NASA's new mission — helping commercial companies develop space taxis for taking astronauts into orbit — is getting less money than the Obama administration requested. Companies like Boeing and SpaceX that are interested in bidding for the work do not yet know whether they can make a profitable venture of it.

When it comes to the future of NASA, "it's hard at this point to speculate," Douglas R. Cooke, associate administrator for NASA's exploration systems mission directorate, said in an interview.

A panel that oversees safety at NASA took note of the uncertainty in its annual report, released this month. "What is NASA's exploration

LUKE SHARRETT/THE NEW YORK TIMES

President Obama toured a launching pad with Elon Musk, the chief executive of Space Exploration Technologies, or SpaceX.

mission?" the members of the Aerospace Safety Advisory Panel asked in their report.

The panel added: "It is not in the nation's best interest to continue functioning in this manner. The Congress, the White House, and NASA must quickly reach a consensus position on the future of the agency and the future of the United States in space."

A nagging worry is that compromises will leave NASA without enough money to accomplish anything, and that — even as billions of dollars are spent — the future destination and schedule of NASA's rockets could turn out to be "nowhere" and "never."

In that case, human spaceflight at NASA would consist just of its work aboard the International Space Station, with the Russians providing the astronaut transportation indefinitely.

"We're on a path with an increasing probability of a bad outcome," said Scott Pace, a former NASA official who now directs the Space Policy Institute at George Washington University.

A NASA study, completed last month, came up with a framework for spaceflight in the two next decades but deferred setting specific destinations, much less timetables for getting there. One of the study's conclusions was that trying to send astronauts to an asteroid by 2025 — as President Obama had challenged the agency to do in a speech last April — was "not prudent," because it would be too expensive and narrow.

Instead, the study advocated a "capability-driven framework" — developing elements like spacecraft, propulsion systems and deep-space living quarters that could be used and reused for a variety of exploration missions.

Meanwhile, in Washington, the fight is less of a conflict of grand visions than a squabble over dollars and the design details of a rocket.

Last fall, in passing an authorization act for NASA, which laid out a blueprint for the next three years, Congress called for NASA to start work on the heavy-lift rocket. It also said that the design should be based on available technologies from the existing space shuttles and from Constellation; that the rocket should be ready by the end of 2016, and that NASA could have about $11.5 billion to develop it.

At the time, Senator Bill Nelson, a Florida Democrat who helped shape the NASA blueprint, said, "If we can't do it for that, then we ought to question whether or not we can build a rocket."

The blueprint, signed into law by President Obama in October, gave NASA 90 days to explain how it would build the rocket.

Two weeks ago, the agency told Congress that it had decided on preferred designs for the rocket and the crew capsule for carrying astronauts, but could not yet fit them into the schedule and constraints.

"All our models say 'no,' " said Elizabeth Robinson, NASA's chief financial officer, "even models that have generous affordability considerations."

She said NASA was continuing to explore how it might reduce costs.

A couple of days after receiving the report, Senator Nelson said he had talked to the NASA administrator, Maj. Gen. Charles F. Bolden Jr., and "told him he has to follow the law, which requires a new rocket by 2016." He added, "And NASA has to do it within the budget the law requires."

The track record for large aerospace development projects, both inside and outside of NASA, is that they almost always take longer and cost more than initially estimated. If costs for the heavy-lift rocket swell, the project could, as Constellation did, divert money from other parts of NASA.

Thus, many NASA observers wonder how the agency can afford to finance both the heavy-lift rocket and the commercial space taxis, which are supposed to begin flying at about the same time.

"They're setting themselves up again for a long development program whose completion is beyond the horizon," James A. M. Muncy, a space policy consultant, said of the current heavy-lift design. "The question is, what does Congress want more? Do they want to just want to keep the contractors on contract, or do they want the United States to explore space?"

He called the situation at NASA "a train wreck," one "where everyone involved knows it's a train wreck."

Constellation, started in 2005 under the Bush administration, aimed to return to the moon by 2020 and set up a base there in the following years. But Constellation never received as much money as originally promised, which slowed work and raised the overall price tag.

When Barack Obama was running for president, he said he supported the moon goal. But after he took office, he did not show much enthusiasm for it. His request for the 2010 fiscal year did not seek immediate cuts in Constellation but trimmed the projected spending in future years.

The administration also set up a blue-ribbon panel, led by Norman Augustine, a former chief executive of Lockheed Martin, to review the program. The panel found that Constellation could not fit into the projected budget — $100 billion over 10 years — and would need $45 billion more to get back on track. Extending the space station five years beyond 2015 would add another $14 billion, the group concluded.

The panel could not find an alternative that would fit, either. It said that for a meaningful human spaceflight program that would push beyond low-Earth orbit, NASA would need $128 billion — $28 billion more than the administration wanted to spend — over the next decade.

If the country was not willing to spend that much, NASA should be asked to do less, the panel said.

Last February, when unveiling the budget request for fiscal year 2011, the Obama administration said it wanted to cancel Constellation, turn to commercial companies for transportation to low-Earth orbit and invest heavily in research and development on technologies for future deep-space missions.

The Obama budget requested more money for NASA — but for other parts of the agency like robotic science missions and aviation. The proposed allotment for human spaceflight was still at levels that the Augustine committee had said were not workable.

In pushing to cancel Constellation, one Obama administration official after another called it "unexecutable," so expensive that it limped along for years without discernible progress.

"The fact that we poured $9 billion into an unexecutable program really isn't an excuse to pour another $50 billion into it and still not have an executable program," said James Kohlenberger, chief of staff of the White House's Office of Science and Technology Policy, at a news conference last February.

At the same news conference, Lori Garver, NASA's deputy administrator, noted that Constellation, without a budget increase, would not reach the moon until well after the 2020 target. "The Augustine report made it clear that we wouldn't have gotten to beyond low Earth orbit until 2028 and even then would not have the funding to build the lander," she said. But with the new road map, NASA may not get to its destinations any faster. As for the ultimate goal of landing people on Mars, which President Obama said he wanted NASA to accomplish by the mid-2030s, it is even slipping further into the future.

Why India Is Going to Mars

OPINION | BY MANOJ KUMAR PATAIRIYA | NOV. 22, 2013

NEW DELHI — If you want to marry in India and are looking for a bride or groom, normally you need to consult an astrologer, to learn whether the position of the planet Mars is favorable on your birth chart. If not, you may find it difficult to get the match of your choice. Lately, some employers have been trying this as well, matching their horoscopes with those of their prospective employees; companies are also comparing horoscopes with their clients for good fortune.

The influence of Mars and the other planets on the life of an average Indian cannot be forgotten, especially this month. On Nov. 5, a Tuesday — Mangalvaar in Hindi, named for the planet Mars — India launched its first mission to the red planet. The day before, the chairman of the Indian Space Research Organization paid a visit to a temple, to seek the blessings of Lord Venkateswara. If the mission is successful, the Mars Orbiter will study the planet's atmosphere and mineralogy, map its surface and test for methane, a possible sign of the presence of life.

Despite significant scientific achievements, many Indians are still guided by superstition, which sometimes is reflected in poor decision making. For example, mothers are often blamed if they do not give birth to a male child. As recently as 2009, the government of Karnataka, a southern state, provided funds to temples for performing religious rituals to nullify the so-called evil effects of a solar eclipse (and this is in the state whose capital, Bangalore, is home to the space research headquarters).

At the same time, the common Indian man is drawn to the country's scientific developments. He is well versed in jugaad — a word we use to describe a kind of traditional, frugal innovation system. The term became popular in the 1990s, and comes from the name of a rural vehicle, designed by villagers who combined an old chassis with an engine commonly used for irrigation pumps. (Today, the Tata Nano car can be seen as an advanced form of jugaad.)

In the years since independence in 1947, when Prime Minister Jawaharlal Nehru called for creating a "scientific temper" among Indian citizens, the government has been investing in science. India has joined the club of the few countries to have mastered the nuclear fuel cycle, from mining to waste disposal. It has designed and operated its own satellites. If the Mars Orbiter successfully reaches the vicinity of the planet in September 2014, after 300 days' journey into deep space, it will make India the first Asian country and the fourth in the world to reach the red planet.

The mission has, however, started an intense debate. While its supporters trumpet its incredibly low cost of around $75 million (a fraction of the cost of a similar American expedition), critics question the logic behind spending any amount when India is dealing with such deep-rooted problems as widespread hunger, poverty and corruption.

One activist, Harsh Mander, said the mission showed a "remarkable indifference to the dignity of the poor."

But U. R. Rao, a former chairman of the Indian Space Research Organization, compared the $75 million spent on the mission to the amount Indians spend on Diwali crackers for one day: "For going all the way to Mars, just one-tenth of the money is being spent. So, why are they shouting?"

Part of the reason the mission is so much less expensive is that it is able to take advantage of existing deep space communications systems and navigation support from NASA. But India is becoming known for its low-cost innovations in many diverse fields, including health care, renewable energy, sanitation, mobile technology and tablet computers. Indian scientists like to share this anecdote: "Americans spent millions to develop a pen that will not leak in space, whereas Russians used a pencil!"

In past decades, an impression was formed that truly innovative research had to be expensive, and "frugal" solutions were written off as low-tech products directed at the poor, says Rajnish Tiwari, a senior researcher at the Institute of Technology and Innovation Management at Hamburg University of Technology. The Mars mission shows that frugal innovations can be high-tech and affordable at the same time.

Many have also dismissed the criticisms by pointing out how much India spends on far less productive projects. For instance, Narendra Modi, the chief minister of the western state of Gujarat and one of the leading contenders for the post of prime minister in next year's elections, has announced the erection of a commemorative statue of Sardar Vallabhbhai Patel, India's first deputy prime minister, that is expected to be double the size of the Statue of Liberty and to cost a whopping $340 million.

The money spent on the Mars mission is a small investment in the big picture. It is a chance to increase the popularity of science and inspire people from all walks of life, both in India and outside.

We still have a long way to go to counter backward superstitions, but we are making progress. During the total solar eclipse of Feb. 16, 1980, most people were too afraid to even come out of their houses. Leading up to the total solar eclipse of Oct. 24, 1995, however, an awareness campaign was carried out, and as a result, many villagers put on solar-filter glasses and joined the scientists to watch the spectacular celestial phenomenon.

I hope that the Mars mission will bring about a greater interest in learning about science, and an end to many of the superstitions associated with the planet. This does not mean that our brides and grooms need to give up all their old beliefs, as there are many aspects of Indian tradition worth preserving. But this too, is possible, for India is a country of contrasts. We know how to embrace two ideas at once — tradition and science, frugality and innovation — just as we can deal with issues like poverty at the same time as taking a giant leap into interplanetary space.

MANOJ KUMAR PATAIRIYA is the editor of the Indian Journal of Science Communication and co-editor of the book "Sharing Science."

On a Shoestring, India Sends Orbiter to Mars on Its First Try

BY GARDINER HARRIS | SEPT. 24, 2014

NEW DELHI — An Indian spacecraft affectionately nicknamed MOM reached Mars orbit on Wednesday, beating India's Asian rivals to the Red Planet and outdoing the Americans, the Soviets and the Europeans in doing so on a maiden voyage and a shoestring budget.

An ebullient Prime Minister Narendra Modi was on hand at the Indian Space Research Organization's command center in Bangalore for the early-morning event and hailed it "as a shining symbol of what we are capable of as a nation."

"The odds were stacked against us," Mr. Modi, wearing a red Nehru vest, said in a televised news conference. "When you are trying to do something that has not been attempted before, it is a leap into the unknown. And space is indeed the biggest unknown out there."

Children across India were asked to come to school by 6:45 a.m. Wednesday, well before the usual starting time, to watch the historic event on state television.

The Mars Orbiter Mission, or MOM, was intended mostly to prove that India could succeed in such a highly technical endeavor — and to beat China. As Mr. Modi and others have noted, India's trip to Mars, at a price of $74 million, cost less than the Hollywood movie "Gravity." NASA's almost simultaneous — and far more complex — mission to Mars cost $671 million.

Success was by no means assured. Of the 51 attempts to reach Mars, only 21 have succeeded, and none on any country's first try, Mr. Modi noted. In 2012, China tried and failed, and in 1999, Japan also failed.

But Mr. Modi, who was elected in May with a once-in-a-generation majority in Parliament, has been on something of a roll. And the Mars achievement, which he had almost nothing to do with, will only add to that.

Mr. Modi leaves Friday for New York, where he will address the United Nations General Assembly as well as a sold-out, largely Indian-American crowd at Madison Square Garden before heading to Washington for a meeting with President Obama.

The Indian Space Research Organization has always had a small budget, and for years it largely worked in international isolation after many countries cut off technological sharing programs in the wake of Indian nuclear tests. It has launched more than 50 satellites since 1975, including five foreign satellites in one June launch. As other countries have rethought their pricey space programs, India's low-budget affair has gained increasing attention and orders.

Its success has long been seen as a fulfillment of the kind of state-sponsored self-sufficiency that former Prime Minister Jawaharlal Nehru cherished but that, in the main, left India impoverished.

More recently, India's technological isolation in defense and other areas has been due in large part to the country's restrictions on foreign investments, its poor infrastructure and its infamous bureaucracy. India is now the world's largest importer of arms because of its inability to make its own equipment and its refusal to let foreign companies open plants owned entirely by them.

The country's most important export is the cheap brainpower of its engineers, based in technology centers like Bangalore and Hyderabad, who provide software and back-office operations for corporations around the world.

"Our success on Mars is a crucial marketing opportunity for low-cost technological know-how, which is what we do really well," said C. Uday Bhaskar, an analyst with the Society for Policy Studies, a New Delhi research center. India's space program "spent peanuts, and they got it done."

India's decision to launch Mangalyaan, the name of its spacecraft, resulted after China's own mission to Mars failed in 2012. In almost every sphere, the Chinese have outpaced the Indians over the past three decades, but Indian scientists saw an opportunity to beat them to Mars.

In just a few months, they cobbled together a mission to send a 33-pound payload of fairly simple sensors to Mars orbit. They used a small rocket, a modest 3,000-pound spacecraft and a plan to slingshot around the Earth to gain the speed needed to get there. A mission that began with a November launch in Sriharikota has been flawless ever since.

"In this Asian space race, India has won the race," Pallava Bagla, author of "Reaching for the Stars: India's Journey to Mars and Beyond," said in an interview.

The triumph was well timed. Thousands of Indian and Chinese soldiers have been engaged in a standoff for more than a week on disputed land in Ladakh, in the Indian-controlled portion of Kashmir, and President Xi Jinping of China recently held a three-day visit to India that was overshadowed by the border disputes.

Mangalyaan, which is the Hindi word for "Mars craft," is slated to remain in an elliptical orbit around Mars, sending back information about Martian weather and methane levels in its atmosphere to controllers in Bangalore from sensors powered by three large solar panels.

SUHASINI RAJ contributed reporting.

Telescope That 'Ate Astronomy' Is on Track to Surpass Hubble

BY DENNIS OVERBYE | NOV. 21, 2016

GREENBELT, MD. — The next great space telescope spread its golden wings this month.

Like the petals of a 20-foot sunflower seeking the light, the 18 hexagonal mirrors that make up the heart of NASA's James Webb Space Telescope were faced toward a glassed-in balcony overlooking a cavernous clean room at the Goddard Space Flight Center here.

Inside the room, reporters and a gaggle of space agency officials, including the ebullient administrator Charles Bolden, were getting their pictures taken in front of the giant mirror.

Now, after 20 years with a budget of $8.7 billion, the Webb telescope is on track and on budget to be launched in October 2018 and sent a million miles from Earth, NASA says.

The telescope, named after NASA Administrator James Webb, who led the space agency in the 1960s, is the long-awaited successor of the Hubble Space Telescope.

Seven times larger than the Hubble in light-gathering ability, the Webb was designed to see farther out in space and deeper into the past of the universe. It may solve mysteries about how and when the first stars and galaxies emerged some 13 billion years ago in the smoky aftermath of the Big Bang.

Equipped with the sort of infrared goggles that give troops and police officers night vision, the Webb would peer into the dust clouds and gas storms of the Milky Way in which stars and planets are presently being birthed. It would be able to study planets around other stars.

That has been NASA's dream since 1996 when the idea for the telescope was conceived with a projected price tag then of $500 million But as recently as six years ago, the James Webb Space Telescope was, in the words of Nature magazine, "the telescope that ate astronomy," mismanaged, over budget and behind schedule so that it had crushed everything else out of NASA's science budget.

A House subcommittee once voted to cancel it. Instead, the program was rebooted with a strict spending cap.

The scientific capabilities of the telescope emerged unscathed from that period, astronomers on the project say. The major change, said Jonathan P. Gardner, the deputy senior project scientist, was to simplify the testing of the telescope.

Most of the pain was dealt to other NASA projects like a proposed space telescope to study dark energy, which the National Academy of Sciences had hoped to put on a fast track to be launched this decade. It's now delayed until 2025 or so.

Typically for NASA, the Webb telescope was a technologically ambitious project, requiring 10 new technologies to make it work. Bill Ochs, a veteran Goddard engineer who became project manager in 2010 during what he calls the "replan," said the key to its success so far, was having enough money in the budget to provide a cushion for nasty surprises.

The telescope smiling up at us like a giant Tiffany shaving mirror is 6.5 meters in diameter, or just over 21 feet, compared with 2.4 meters for the Hubble. The aim is to explore a realm of cosmic history about 150 million to one billion years after time began — known as the reionization epoch, when bright and violent new stars and the searing radiation from quasars were burning away a gloomy fog of hydrogen gas that prevailed at the end of the Big Bang.

In fact, astronomers don't know how the spectacle that greets our eyes every night when the sun goes down or the lights go out wrenched itself into luminous existence. They theorize that an initial generation of stars made purely of hydrogen and helium — the elements created during the Big Bang — burned ferociously and exploded apocalyptically, jump-starting the seeding of the cosmos with progressively more diverse materials. But nobody has ever seen any so-called Population 3 stars, as those first stars are known.

They don't exist in the modern universe. Astronomers have to hunt them in the dim past.

That ambition requires the Webb to be tuned to a different kind of light than our eyes or the Hubble can see. Because the expansion of the cosmos is rushing those earliest stars and galaxies away from us so fast, their light is "red-shifted" to longer wavelengths the way the siren from an ambulance shifts to a lower register as it passes by.

So blue light from an infant galaxy bursting with bright spanking new stars way back then has been stretched to invisible infrared wavelengths, or heat radiation, by the time it reaches us 13 billion years later.

As a result, the Webb telescope will produce cosmic postcards in colors no eye has ever seen. It also turns out that infrared emanations are the best way to study exoplanets, the worlds beyond our own solar system that have been discovered in the thousands since the Webb telescope was first conceived.

In order to see those infrared colors, however, the telescope has to be very cold — less than 45 degrees Fahrenheit above absolute zero — so that its own heat does not swamp the heat from outer space. Once in space, the telescope will unfold a giant umbrella the size of a tennis court to keep the sun off it. The telescope, marooned in permanent shade a million miles beyond the moon, will experience an infinite cold soak.

The sunshield consists of five thin, kite-shaped layers of a material called Kapton. Way too big to fit into a rocket, the shield, as well as the telescope mirror, will have be launched folded up. It will then be unfolded in space in a series of some 180 maneuvers that look in computer animations like a cross between a parachute opening and a swimming pool cover going into place.

Or at least that is the $8 billion plan.

Engineers have done it on the ground, and it worked. The same people who refolded the shield after each test will fold it again, in a process Mr. Ochs compares to packing up your parachute before a jump. The test will come in space, where no one will be able to help if things go wrong.

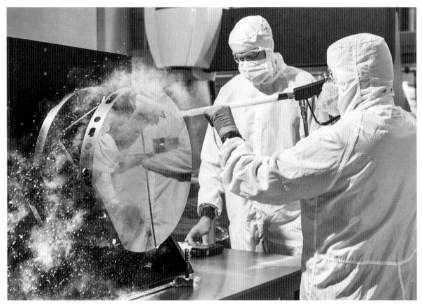

Two Exelis Inc. engineers practicing "snow cleaning" on a test mirror for the James Webb Space Telescope.

That whole process will amount to what Mr. Ochs called "six months of high anxiety."

"For the most part, it all has to work," Mr. Ochs said.

The last time NASA did something this big astronomically, in 1990, things didn't quite work. Once in orbit, the Hubble couldn't be focused; it had a misshapen mirror that had never been properly tested. Astronauts eventually fitted it with corrective lenses, and it went on to become the crown jewel of astronomy.

Making sure that doesn't happen this time is the agenda for the next two years. "Our telescope is finished," John C. Mather, the senior project scientist, said. "Now we are about to prove it works."

In the coming weeks, the mirror and the box of scientific instruments on its back will be put on a rig and shaken to simulate the vibrations of a launch, and then sealed in an acoustic chamber and bombarded with the noise of a launch.

If the parts survive unscathed, the telescope assembly will be shipped to a giant vacuum chamber at the Johnson Space Center in Houston. There it will be chilled to the deep-space temperatures at which it will have to work, and engineers will actually focus the telescope, twiddling the controls for seven actuators on each of the 18 mirror segments. No Hubble surprises here.

Then the telescope will go to Los Angeles to be mounted on its gigantic sunshield. That whole contraption, now too big for even the giant C-5A military transport plane, will travel by ship through the Panama Canal to French Guiana.

It will be launched on an Ariane 5 rocket supplied by the European Space Agency as part of Europe's contribution to the observatory, and go into orbit around the sun at a point called L2 about a million miles from Earth. Canada, NASA's other partner, supplied some of the instruments.

Then come the six months of anxiety. Sometime in the spring of 2019, if all goes well, the telescope will record its first real image — of what, the assembled astronomers were not ready to guess. In a bonus undreamed of when the Webb telescope was first conceived, it looks as if the Hubble will still be going strong when the Webb is launched. They will share the sky and the potential for joint observing projects. A million miles apart, they can view objects in the solar system from different angles, providing a kind of stereoscopic perspective.

Besides the expected baby galaxies and the exoplanets, there are, as astronomers like to remind us, always new surprises (like colliding black holes when the LIGO observatory was turned on last year) when humanity devises a new way to look at the sky.

Asked what the telescope's greatest discovery would be, Dr. Mather said, "If I knew, I would tell you."

Nor would the project members talk about contingency plans to rescue the telescope if anything goes wrong a million miles from Earth. There are no plans to fix it or bring it back. They know how to attach a probe or robot to the telescope, Dr. Mather said, but "we are planning to not need it, thank you."

Space Council Chooses the Moon as Trump Administration Priority

BY KENNETH CHANG | OCT. 5, 2017

CHANTILLY, VA. — Standing before the space shuttle Discovery in a voluminous hangar outside of Washington, Vice President Mike Pence announced on Thursday a renewed focus on putting Americans in space and making a return to the moon.

"We will return American astronauts to the moon, not only to leave behind footprints and flags, but to build the foundation we need to send Americans to Mars and beyond," Mr. Pence said during a meeting of the National Space Council.

The council, a group of senior federal officials that coordinates policy between NASA, the Defense Department and other agencies involved with space, was disbanded in 1993, but President Trump signed an executive order in June to reestablish it. (The meeting, which was held at the National Air & Space Museum's Steven F. Udvar-Hazy Center, was streamed live on the internet).

Council members include Secretary of State Rex Tillerson; Secretary of Transportation Elaine Chao; Secretary of Commerce Wilbur Ross; General H.R. McMaster, the national security adviser; and Mike Mulvaney, director of the Office of Management and Budget.

Mr. Pence did not lay out a timetable for when American astronauts would step on the moon again or propose a strategy for getting there, much less broach the topic of a price tag.

In his introductory comments to the council, Mr. Pence described the United States space program as in decline, and leveled sharp criticism of the Obama administration. "Rather than competing with other nations to create the best space technology, the previous administration chose capitulation," he said.

"Have we fallen behind as we believe?" Mr. Pence asked private sector aerospace executives speaking at the session. "Is that your judgment from the outside?"

The executives largely sidestepped the question.

"I would say, first of all, that is very important today, that it is an imperative," said Marillyn A. Hewson, chief executive of Lockheed Martin. She said that there was a need to be "vigilant" about protecting communications and intelligence satellites from attack, but then pivoted to talking about the economic, educational and inspirational benefits of the space program.

She and Dennis A. Muilenburg, chief executive of Boeing, both said there was a need for consistent financing and steady commitment to achieve long-term objectives in space.

Officials from newer space companies, Elon Musk's SpaceX and Jeffrey P. Bezos's Blue Origin, called for public-private partnerships rather than traditional government-run programs and called for streamlining the bureaucratic process of licensing launches.

Gwynne Shotwell, president of SpaceX, far from describing a neglected space program in the United States, highlighted her company's meteoric rise in recent years, with 13 launches in 2017. "In short, there is a renaissance underway right now in space," she said.

The focus on the moon marks an expected turn from the priorities of the Obama administration, which had downplayed the moon and instructed NASA to instead aim for an asteroid and then Mars. The approach is more of a return to the path described by President George W. Bush in 2004 and his father, President George H.W. Bush, 15 years earlier.

Both times, the initiatives petered out. Since the last Apollo moon landing in 1972, no astronauts have traveled beyond low-Earth orbit.

Mr. Pence suggested that private industry might play a larger role in a moon mission this time. "To fully unlock the mysteries of space, President Trump recognizes that we must look beyond the halls of government for input and guidance," he said.

In a Wall Street Journal opinion article published on Wednesday where Mr. Pence addressed similar themes, he made zero mention of NASA.

What will change in practice under the Trump administration is unclear. Although the Obama administration downplayed sending NASA astronauts to the moon, it did support commercial start-ups seeking to send robotic landers there, and Mr. Pence said that the longer-term goal of getting astronauts to Mars remains.

Phillip Larson, a former White House space adviser in the Obama administration and now an assistant dean at the University of Colorado engineering school disagreed with Mr. Pence's criticism. He pointed to SpaceX's success and billions of dollars of private investment in space ventures in recent years.

"That type of activity is what the Obama administration worked to promote and create and foment a whole new industry," said Mr. Larson, who did not attend the meeting.

He said it was also too early to tell whether the Trump administration's space efforts would succeed. "It was just very interesting to do this type of process without a NASA administrator or a science adviser in the White House," he said. "Until they produce a plan, which it looks like they're moving toward, this is mostly theater and produces a little bit of confusion, I think. I still remain optimistic."

The Senate has not yet held confirmation hearings for Jim Bridenstine, an Oklahoma congressman nominated last month to be the next NASA administrator. President Trump has yet to name a science adviser.

John Logsdon, a former director of the Space Policy Institute at George Washington University, was more positive, noting that the administration had chosen to hold its first meeting publicly at a high-profile venue to draw more attention.

"Words are the first step to action," he said.

Are the words different this time?

Dr. Logsdon paused. "No," he replied wistfully.

As America Looks Inward, China Looks to Outer Space

BY MIKE IVES | MAY 23, 2018

HONG KONG — While President Trump refocuses American industry on the earthbound technologies of the 20th century — coal, steel and aluminum — China is setting its sights on the far reaches of the solar system.

China this week launched a rocket headed for the moon, where for now only an American flag flies, with ambitions to land a spacecraft on its unexplored far side by the end of the year.

Trippy as a visit to the "dark side" of the moon sounds, it is just the most recent mission by the Chinese to advance their space program and supplant the United States as the front-runner in the space race.

Chinese plans include putting a person on the moon and sending a mission to Mars by 2025. Here's a look at some of China's boldest recent endeavors.

VISITING THE DARK SIDE OF THE MOON

China on Monday launched a relay satellite, a pivotal first step toward ensuring that controllers could land an unmanned spacecraft on the moon's far side later this year.

The far side of the moon does not face the Earth, hindering communications with earthbound scientists, and making its previous exploration virtually impossible.

A successful mission would be a significant scientific achievement as well as useful propaganda tool for President Xi Jinping, who sees China's largely military-run space program as a vehicle for enhancing national prestige.

A 'RABBIT' DISCOVERS MOON ROCKS

While China's mission to the dark side of the moon would be a first for the world, Chinese spacecraft have previously visited the moon.

In 2013, the year Mr. Xi first assumed power, China became the third country — after the United States and the Soviet Union — to steer a spacecraft onto the moon. The rover known as Jade Rabbit operated for more than two years, and allowed researchers to investigate the moon's surface remotely using spectrometers, and discover a new type of basaltic rock.

A year later, an unmanned Chinese spacecraft orbited the moon to test equipment and techniques for a future lunar mission. It carried a microchip with Chinese music, including a song by Peng Liyuan, a famous singer who is married to Mr. Xi.

Mr. Xi has said the target date for sending an astronaut to the moon is 2025.

CHINA JOINS THE ASTRONAUT CLUB

China is also only the third country to send its own astronauts to space aboard its own rocket.

The country conducted its first manned mission to space in 2003, and has since sent several other astronauts and put a pair of space stations into orbit.

In 2016, China sent two astronauts to space for 30 days, its longest manned mission to date. The mission was China's sixth human space launch, and the two astronauts more than doubled the national record for staying in space.

The astronauts docked with a space station, where they conducted experiments in a lab, as well as testing computer, propulsion and life support systems, according to state news media.

A MISSION TO MARS ... AND BEYOND

China plans to deploy a rover to Mars by 2020, state news media reported in 2016. The rover would carry a remote sensing camera and ground-penetrating radar capable of studying the planet's soil and water, among other things.

China also plans to "probe asteroids" around 2022, bring Martian samples back to Earth in 2028 and send an exploratory mission to Jupiter around 2029, a top official at the National Space Administration told the state news agency Xinhua in April.

And by 2050, he added, China wants to have a lunar research station that would be operated by robots and visited occasionally by astronauts.

THE WORLD'S BIGGEST RADIO TELESCOPE

In 2016, China completed construction on the world's largest single-dish radio telescope. Likened to a giant wok, astronomers use the telescope, located in Guizhou Province, to chart the shape of the universe and even listen for potential signs of alien life.

Other recent advancements include the launch of the world's first quantum communications satellite, which promises to improve the security of communications by sending information on photons of light.

KAROLINE KAN contributed research from Beijing.

NASA Names Astronauts for Boeing and SpaceX Flights to International Space Station

BY KAREN ZRAICK | AUG. 3, 2018

NASA HAS NAMED the astronauts chosen to fly on commercial spacecraft made by Boeing and SpaceX to and from the International Space Station, the research laboratory that orbits around Earth.

Their voyages are scheduled to begin next year, and they would be the first American astronauts to launch from United States soil since 2011. NASA retired its space shuttle fleet that year, and started sending astronauts to the I.S.S. aboard the Russian Soyuz spacecraft, at a cost that has risen to $81 million per seat.

"What an exciting and amazing day," Jim Bridenstine, NASA's administrator, said at the announcement at NASA's Johnson Space Center in Houston.

But a Government Accountability Office report published last month raised alarm bells that the project is running behind schedule, and could miss key deadlines. The delays could even result in a gap in American access to the space station, because NASA has contracted for seats on Soyuz only through November 2019, the report found.

On Friday, NASA said that if uncrewed test flights go smoothly, the astronauts will fly before then, on roughly two-week test flights and later on missions of Boeing's CST-100 Starliner and SpaceX's Crew Dragon. NASA worked closely with the companies to engineer both spacecraft.

"The opportunity to fly in a new vehicle is any test pilot and astronaut's dream," Mike Hopkins, an Air Force colonel who will fly aboard the Crew Dragon on its first long-term mission, wrote on Twitter. Such missions usually last five to six months.

Colonel Hopkins had previously spent 166 days on the I.S.S., and conducted two spacewalks. He'll be joined by Victor Glover, a Navy commander who will be making his first trip into space.

The test flight astronauts on the Crew Dragon, both of whom joined NASA in 2000, will be Col. Bob Behnken of the Air Force and Doug Hurley, a retired Marine Corps colonel. The Crew Dragon will launch aboard a Falcon 9 rocket from the Kennedy Space Center in Florida. The uncrewed test is planned for November; the test flight with crew aboard is set for April 2019.

The astronauts assigned to the Starliner's first mission are Sunita Williams, who retired as a Navy captain, and Cmdr. Josh Cassada of the Navy, who will be making his first voyage into space.

Captain Williams has spent 322 days aboard the I.S.S. since becoming an astronaut in 1998. While she was there in 2007, she completed the Boston Marathon — on a treadmill — in 4 hours 24 minutes, marking the first time an entrant had finished the race from orbit.

On the test flight for the Starliner will be: Eric Boe, a former space shuttle pilot who retired from the Air Force; Christopher Ferguson, a Boeing astronaut who left NASA in 2011; and Lt. Col. Nicole Mann of the Marine Corps. It would be the first space trip for Colonel Mann.

The Starliner will launch aboard an Atlas V rocket from Cape Canaveral Air Force Station. The uncrewed test flight is scheduled for late 2018 or early 2019. The test flight with crew is scheduled for mid-2019.

Douglas Stanley, head of the National Institute of Aerospace in Hampton, Va., said it's crucial for the United States not to depend on Russia to conduct space research.

"We're very pleased to see it happen," he said. "We think its very important for the nation to have a domestic capability to launch astronauts."

Maintaining the I.S.S. costs the federal government up to $4 billion a year, and NASA is working on plans to privatize it. The Trump administration proposed eliminating direct federal funding for the

facing a commercial market with a range of entrepreneurs who say they can do that work for less.

Under Mr. Obama's ambitious initiative, NASA would rely on commercial companies to provide a kind of taxi service to the International Space Station, while focusing its efforts on missions into deep space with international partners.

How the aerospace industry establishment will fit into this new plan remains far from clear, analysts say.

"I see a certain analogy with what happened when computers went from being room-sized to being on the desktop," said Louis D. Friedman, executive director for Planetary Society, a space exploration advocacy group.

"Some companies barely survived, while others adapted and thrived. I think we are going to see something like this in the aerospace industry."

The most immediate effect of the proposed policy shift will be on jobs. Mr. Obama's plan to cancel the Constellation program, started five years ago by President George W. Bush to send astronauts back to the moon, could mean the end of nearly 12,600 jobs, according to estimates by aerospace contractors. The cuts would fall most heavily on Alabama, California, Florida, Texas and Utah, and political opposition from those states has been vociferous.

The Constellation program has already cost American taxpayers about $9 billion.

The end of Constellation would largely stop work on the Ares I rocket, which was to replace the space shuttle for carrying astronauts into orbit and would scale back work on the Orion crew capsule, which was to ride atop the Ares I. Lockheed Martin said more than 2,000 jobs depended on the Orion program, while Boeing said 1,500 jobs would be affected by the retirement of the space shuttle and the canceling of Constellation. Alliant Techsystems, known as ATK, said the ending of Ares I would put 5,000 jobs at risk at its plants and those of its subcontractors.

Mr. Obama has said that the changes do not amount to a retreat from manned spaceflight and that adding private entrepreneurs to the mix will create a more vibrant industry with more astronauts in space and more business for established companies and newcomers alike.

One established player that appears to accept Mr. Obama's plan is United Launch Alliance, a 50-50 joint venture of Boeing and Lockheed Martin. The company, whose Atlas and Delta rockets have carried military and commercial satellites into space for decades, said it had no plans to cut any jobs.

"Just the opposite," a U.L.A. spokesman said.

"The president's new plan could have a significant increase in demand coming from NASA and could create new jobs at U.L.A.," the spokesman said, adding that U.L.A.'s long record of successful launchings made it "very different from new entrants."

One new entrant much on the minds of the aerospace community is Space Exploration Technologies, founded by Elon Musk, the Internet entrepreneur who helped found the payment system PayPal. The company, which did not exist a decade ago, has $2.5 billion in contracts, including $1.6 billion from NASA to provide a minimum of 12 flights to deliver cargo to the space station starting in 2011.

The company, known as SpaceX, bolstered the credibility of Mr. Obama's plan by launching into orbit last month the Falcon 9, a rocket measuring 158 feet, or 48 meters, and weighing 735,000 pounds, or 335,000 kilograms. The rocket, which the company said cost about $50 million, put a model of its Dragon capsule into orbit about 160 miles, or 260 kilometers, above the Earth without a hitch — an unusual development for a maiden flight.

SpaceX, which plans to launch a fully operational rocket and capsule this summer before sending one to the International Space Station next year, said the successful June trial was a major victory "for NASA's plan to use commercial rockets for astronaut transport."

The part of Mr. Obama's plan that calls for missions that leave the Earth's orbit to explore deep space will probably not be spelled out for several years. Mr. Obama has said that NASA will start developing a heavy-lift rocket for deep-space missions by 2015.

That gap of several years between the planned end of the Constellation program and the start of work on a new heavy-lift vehicle does not please the aerospace contractors, who say they could shift at least some workers who might otherwise be laid off into a new deep-space program. It is also dangerous, some analysts say, because after canceling the Ares I, the United States would have no backup rocket if new commercial companies failed to deliver on their promises.

"It's a risky strategy," said Loren B. Thompson, an analyst at the Lexington Institute, a research group financed in part by military contractors. "Our capacity to send man-rated rockets into space is at risk."

In a statement in response to Mr. Obama's April 15 speech at the Kennedy Space Center in Florida outlining his new policy, Boeing emphasized the need for immediate development of a heavy-lift vehicle.

"We have the technology and the people to commence development of these vehicles now," Boeing said. Accelerated development of a deep-space launching vehicle and capsule "could achieve maximum benefit for American tax dollars by drawing on the cutting-edge technology already being developed for the Constellation program," Boeing said.

John M. Logsdon, the former director of the Space Policy Institute at George Washington University, said he had no doubt that NASA would contract for a heavy-lift vehicle sometime in the next few years and that the traditional aerospace companies would get the bulk of this work.

"But in the short-term, they stand to lose the contracts for Constellation and all that goes with it," he said "They are trading contracts in hand for some very uncertain contracts in the future."

Not a Flight of Fancy

OPINION | BY SAM HOWE VERHOVEK | NOV. 3, 2014

SEATTLE — One clear winter day in 1909, in Hampshire, England, a young man named Geoffrey de Havilland took off in a twin-propeller motorized flying machine of his own design, built of wood, piano wire and stiff linen hand-stitched by his wife. The launch was flawless, and soon he had an exhilarating sensation of climbing almost straight upward toward the brilliant blue sky. But he soon realized he was in terrible trouble.

The angle of ascent was unsustainable, and moments later de Havilland's experimental plane crashed, breaking apart into a tangled mass of shards, splinters and torn fabric, lethal detritus that could easily have killed him even if the impact of smashing into the ground did not. Somehow, he survived and Sir Geoffrey — he was ultimately knighted as one of the world's great aviation pioneers — went on to build an astonishing array of military and civilian aircraft, including the world's first jet airliner, the de Havilland Comet.

I thought immediately of de Havilland on Friday when I heard that Virgin Galactic's SpaceShipTwo, a rocket-powered vehicle designed to take well-heeled tourists to the edge of space, had crashed on a flight over the Mojave Desert, killing one test pilot and seriously injuring the other. The in-air "anomaly," as it was first described in a company Twitter posting, comes on top of an explosion in 2007 during a rocket-fuel test that killed three employees on the ground at the Mojave Air and Space Port.

These sacrifices were not just tragic; to many people there was something needless or even obscene about them. Brave men are dead in service of a for-profit venture in which a bunch of thrill-seeking billionaires and Hollywood A-listers have plunked down deposits up to the full $250,000 cost for a ticket to slip the surly bonds for several minutes of floating weightlessness and trophy photography 62 miles above the Earth, at the very edge of our atmosphere. For some whose job it was to make that happen, this has truly been a view to die for.

But whether or not Friday's crash was preventable, it was far from pointless. It is worth considering that to a striking degree, the criticism of "space tourism" today echoes the scoffing of a century ago that greeted the arrival of powered flight.

Certainly the Wright brothers and others like de Havilland were involved in what we now view as an epic quest, but many experts of the day were certain that flight, however interesting, was destined to be not much more than a rich man's hobby with no practical value.

"The public has greatly over-estimated the possibilities of the aeroplane, imagining that in another generation they will be able to fly over to London in a day," said a Harvard expert in 1908. "This is manifestly impossible." Two other professors patiently explained that while laymen might think that "because a machine will carry two people another may be constructed that will carry a dozen," in fact "those who make this contention do not understand the theory of weight sustentation in the air."

In recent years I have interviewed a wide array of people involved in the private space industry, including both pilots involved in the crash on Friday. Almost universally, they viewed themselves as pioneers at the dawn of an era of exploration whose apogee is beyond our generation's imagination. Just as the Wright brothers did not have a precise image in mind of jumbo jetliners ferrying people around the world so routinely and so safely at more than 500 miles per hour that we have long since stopped considering it a miracle, we can't really know where we're headed in space.

But, they insist, we certainly need to go there. "I think it is actually very important that we start making progress in extending life beyond Earth and we start making our own existence a multi-planetary one," Elon Musk, the founder of SpaceX (its goal: "enabling people to live on other planets") once told me. He called the venture a "giant insurance policy" for the survival of our species. Seen in this light, the first round of space tourism is simply seed capital for something much grander.

JOHNNY SAMPSON

It's possible that tomorrow's budget-minded space travelers will thank today's 1-percenters, just as you can credit early adopters of expensive, behemoth mainframe computers for your $250 desktop.

One could argue, of course, that space tourism is more grandiose than grand. After all, one of the enduring ironies of the initial space age is that we spent all those billions of dollars to produce, among other things, magnificent and iconic remote photographs of Earth that fired the environmental movement to focus on protecting our lonely, beautiful, fragile blue island of a planet.

And as a general matter, we are less excited about the possibilities of space exploration than we were a half-century ago. But if we are ever to reach Mars, or colonize an asteroid or find new minerals in outer space, today's work will prove to have been a vital link in the chain.

There will be tragedies like the crash of SpaceShipTwo and nonlethal setbacks such as the fiery explosion, also last week, of a remote-controlled rocket intended for a resupply mission to the International Space Station. There will be debates about how to improve regulation without stifling innovation. Some will say private industry can't do the job — though it's not as if the NASA-sponsored Apollo or space shuttle missions went off without a hitch (far from it, sadly).

But at the heart of the enterprise there will always be obsessives like Sir Geoffrey, who forged ahead with his life's work of building airplanes despite his own crash and, incredibly, the deaths of two of his three sons while piloting de Havilland aircraft, one in an attempt to break the sound barrier. Getting to routine safety aloft claimed many lives along the way, and a hundred years from now people will agree that in that regard, at least, spaceships are no different from airplanes.

SAM HOWE VERHOVEK, a former New York Times correspondent, is the author of "Jet Age: The Comet, the 707, and the Race to Shrink the World."

Virgin Galactic SpaceShipTwo Crash Traced to Co-Pilot Error

BY KENNETH CHANG | JULY 28, 2015

A SINGLE MISTAKE by the co-pilot led to the fatal disintegration of a Virgin Galactic space plane during a test flight in October, the National Transportation Safety Board concluded Tuesday, and the board strongly criticized the company that designed and manufactured the plane for not building safeguards into the controls and procedures.

"Many of the safety issues that we will hear about today arose not from the novelty of a space launch test flight," the board's chairman, Christopher A. Hart, said during a hearing in Washington, "but from human factors that were already known elsewhere in transportation."

The safety board was also critical of the Federal Aviation Administration for not following up on issues that could result in mistakes by pilots.

The craft, called SpaceShipTwo, is designed to be carried aloft under a larger aircraft, then dropped before its rocket ignites and propels it upward. Near the top of its ascent, two tail booms rotate upward into a "feathered" position. That is meant to create drag and stability, allowing the plane to descend gently back into the atmosphere, much like a badminton shuttlecock.

Before the accident, the company, Scaled Composites of Mojave, Calif., founded by Burt Rutan, a renowned aerospace engineer, and now part of Northrop Grumman, knew that early rotating of the tail booms could be catastrophic, but its analysis considered only the possibility of mechanical failure, not that a pilot might release the lock on the booms by mistake, investigators said.

Scaled did not include a warning in the operating handbook or add a mechanism to ensure that could not happen. Investigators said the company had placed more concern on unlocking the feathering mechanism too late, also potentially dangerous.

Virgin Galactic, founded by Richard Branson, aims to fly tourists to the edge of space, providing a few minutes of weightlessness, for $250,000 a ticket. It hired Scaled to develop, build and test a suborbital space plane. During Scaled's fourth powered flight of SpaceShipTwo on Oct. 31, the co-pilot, Michael Alsbury, released the feather lock at the speed of Mach 0.82 as it rocketed upward instead of waiting until Mach 1.4, as specified in the procedure, when it would have been much higher in a thinner atmosphere.

The force of the air against SpaceShipTwo's tail caused the tail booms to pivot upward, and the craft broke apart.

Mr. Alsbury was killed. The pilot, Peter Siebold, survived after being thrown out of SpaceShipTwo while still restrained to his seat. Mr. Siebold was able to unbuckle himself before his parachute automatically deployed.

Cockpit video that showed Mr. Alsbury moving the lever to unlock the feather lock too early led investigators to look closely at the training of the pilots and the design of the controls.

"Would a single-point mechanical failure with catastrophic consequences be acceptable?" Robert L. Sumwalt, one of the safety board members, asked the investigators Tuesday.

It would not, answered Michael Hauf, part of the investigation team that spent nine months looking into the crash.

"So why would a single-point human failure be acceptable?" Mr. Sumwalt asked. "And it really should not be acceptable. The fact is, if you put all your eggs in the basket of a human to do it correctly — and I don't mean this flippantly, because I've made plenty of mistakes — humans will screw up anything if you give them enough opportunity. The mistake is often a symptom of a flawed system."

The safety board laid the primary blame on Scaled, describing the probable cause as "Scaled Composites's failure to consider and protect against the possibility that a single human error could result in a catastrophic hazard to the SpaceShipTwo vehicle."

The investigators said that both pilots were qualified and that no health problems or mechanical malfunctions had played a role.

Scaled issued a statement on Tuesday saying that safety was a "critical component" of the company's culture. "As part of our constant and continuing efforts to enhance our processes, we have already made changes in the wake of the accident to further enhance safety."

The safety board issued 10 recommendations, most directed at the F.A.A.

In 2013, before renewing Scaled's permit for operating Space-ShipTwo, the F.A.A.'s Office of Commercial Space Transportation identified shortcomings in Scaled's analysis of human factors and computer software. But without Scaled asking, it granted a waiver to those permit requirements, and Scaled did not redo its analysis.

At present, the F.A.A.'s responsibility in private spaceflight is to ensure that launchings do not endanger people on the ground, not to certify the design of spacecraft.

Referring to the F.A.A., Katherine A. Wilson, an investigator for the safety board, said, "There seemed to be a disconnect between the information that staff wanted, the technical information, and management, which believed that those questions were not relevant to public safety."

Virgin Galactic, not Scaled, is building a second SpaceShipTwo, and it hopes to resume ground and flight tests in the coming months. An automatic mechanism has been added to prevent the feathering from being unlocked early.

Elon Musk's Plan: Get Humans to Mars, and Beyond

BY KENNETH CHANG | SEPT. 27, 2016

GUADALAJARA, MEXICO — Elon Musk's plans to get to Mars start with a really big rocket. He still needs to figure out how to pay for it.

For years, Mr. Musk, the billionaire founder of the SpaceX rocket company, has been offering hints and teases of his desire to colonize the big red planet.

In a talk on Tuesday at the International Astronautical Congress here, Mr. Musk finally provided engineering details, optimistic timelines and a slick video.

"What you saw there is very close to what we'll actually build," Mr. Musk said, referring to the rockets and spacecraft in the video.

Mr. Musk estimated it would cost $10 billion to develop the rocket, and he said the first passengers to Mars could take off as soon as 2024 if the plans went off without a hitch. For now, SpaceX is financing development costs of a few tens of millions of dollars a year, but eventually the company would look to some kind of public-private partnership.

Each of the SpaceX vehicles would take 100 passengers on the journey to Mars, with trips planned every 26 months, when Earth and Mars pass close to each other. Tickets per person might cost $500,000 at first, and drop to about a third of that later on, Mr. Musk said.

To establish a self-sustaining Mars civilization of a million people would take 10,000 flights, with many more to ferry equipment and supplies.

"We're going to need something quite large to do that," Mr. Musk said. It would take 40 years to a century before the city on Mars became self-sufficient, he said.

The mood at the conference was almost as giddy as a rock concert or the launch of a new Apple product, with people lining up for Mr. Musk's presentation a couple of hours in advance.

Mr. Musk has talked of his "Mars Colonial Transporter," but a couple of weeks ago, he suggested that its capabilities would be much greater.

He now calls it the Interplanetary Transport System. The booster would include 42 of SpaceX's new, more powerful Raptor engines. On Monday, he posted an image on Twitter of the first testing of a Raptor.

Mars has long been the goal of Mr. Musk and SpaceX.

Much of Mr. Musk's initial wealth came from his tenure as chief executive of PayPal, which he sold to eBay in 2002 for $1.5 billion. Afterward, he wanted to undertake a science experiment — to send a greenhouse to Mars and see if Earth plants could grow in Martian dirt. He said the rocket options for launching his project were so lacking that he started SpaceX, which has headquarters in Hawthorne, Calif.

SpaceX has established a successful business with its workhorse Falcon 9 rocket launching satellites, and by taking cargo — and soon astronauts — to the International Space Station for NASA. But Mr. Musk has stated often that his loftier goal for SpaceX is to send people to Mars to make humanity a "multiplanetary species" in order to ensure survival in case some calamity like an asteroid strike befell Earth.

The new rocket could be used for even more distant trips, to places like Europa, the icy moon of Jupiter.

"This system really gives you freedom to go anywhere you want in the greater solar system," he said.

What is less clear is how SpaceX will raise the money needed to bring its Mars dreams to fruition. The new rocket is by far the largest ever.

Scott Pace, a former NASA official who is the director of the Space Policy Institute at George Washington University, said Mr. Musk's vision was plausible technically, but added, "Other than emotional appeal, however, it didn't really address why governments, corporations or other organizations would fund the effort." His bottom-line opinion: "Possible, but not probable."

During his talk, Mr. Musk put up a slide titled "Funding." The first item was "Steal underpants," a joking reference to a "South Park" episode. He also listed SpaceX's businesses — launching satellites and sending NASA cargo and astronauts to the space station — and "Kickstarter."

But he admitted that SpaceX would probably not be able to do it alone. "Ultimately, this is going to be a huge public-private partnership," he said.

SpaceX has received much of the financing for its rocket development from NASA, from contracts to take cargo to and from the International Space Station. The United States Air Force is providing $33.6 million for development of the Raptor.

Critics of SpaceX and Mr. Musk question whether the Mars dreams are distracting the company from its more mundane business. SpaceX's Falcon 9 rocket is grounded while investigators try to figure out why one of the rockets on the launchpad exploded this month during fueling before a test firing.

On Friday, the company said the failure appeared to be a large breach in the helium system of the second stage, although what caused the breach is not known. However, the company said the investigation had ruled out any connection to the failure last year of a Falcon 9 that disintegrated in flight. (That failure was traced to a faulty strut in the second stage, and SpaceX resumed launching later in the year.)

Mr. Musk also faces competition from other billionaires with ambitious space dreams. Jeff Bezos, the founder of Amazon, has his own rocket company, Blue Origin, which this month also announced a new rocket, New Glenn, that approaches the Saturn 5 in stature, but is dwarfed by SpaceX's new rocket.

At a talk here, Robert Meyerson, Blue Origin's president, said the aim of New Glenn was to take people to space, although it will also be able to launch satellites. The images the company released showed the satellite-carrying version. But Mr. Meyerson disclosed that "there are other versions that will have a space vehicle on top."

Mr. Meyerson said Blue Origin had an even larger rocket, to be called New Armstrong, on the drawing board. Mr. Bezos has said his goal is for millions of people to live in space, although he has not mentioned Mars as a destination.

With Mr. Bezos' Amazon wealth, Blue Origin faces less pressure to be profitable as quickly as SpaceX, or public companies like Boeing and Lockheed Martin that have to answer to shareholders.

NASA is still talking about its Mars ambitions, too, and its own giant rocket, the Space Launch System, for eventual human missions there. William H. Gerstenmaier, the associate administrator for human exploration and operations, said all of the pieces for a crewed Mars mission were in development, at least to reach Mars orbit, by the 2030s and fit within the agency's existing budget. "We don't think we're going to get a big new budget," he said.

He admitted that in NASA's plans, astronauts' setting foot on Mars would take longer, probably not until the 2040s.

Mr. Musk was confident that his company could pull off his vision, but he said he would not be among the first colonists, saying he wants to see his children grow up. The chances of dying on that first trip to Mars, he said, are "quite high."

Moon Express Sets Its Sights on Deliveries to the Moon and Beyond

BY KENNETH CHANG | JULY 12, 2017

A FLORIDA START-UP that is striving to become the first private company to put a spacecraft on the moon revealed an ambitious road map on Wednesday for a regular delivery service to send payloads there and elsewhere in the solar system.

Moon Express of Cape Canaveral, Fla., was founded in 2010 to win the Google Lunar X Prize, a competition offering a $20 million prize for the first private venture to get to the moon with a robotic lander by the end of 2017.

Robert D. Richards, the company's chief executive, said Moon Express was on track to launch before the prize's deadline. But even if the company does not win the prize, he said, Moon Express would still have a profitable future ferrying payloads for NASA and commercial customers.

"I think it's big," Dr. Richards said of the potential market, adding that he hoped its designs would "redefine the possible."

The company released illustrations of its MX-1E lander, which it says will make the trip to the moon this year.

An earlier doughnut-shape design is now taller and thinner, about 3 feet wide and 4› feet tall, more like a soda can with landing legs. Julie Arnold, a spokeswoman for Moon Express, said the lander would be a little bigger than the R2-D2 robot from the movie "Star Wars."

The design change was made so that the lander would fit in a smaller rocket that Moon Express now plans to use for the first mission. "That's considered our starter vehicle, our entry-level vehicle, to reach the moon," Dr. Richards said.

The MX-1E then becomes like a Lego piece, allowing Moon Express to use it as a building block for larger spacecraft.

"Space vehicles and landers have traditionally been custom designed for each purpose," Dr. Richards said. "What we've designed is a common core approach."

Moon Express's second mission would use a larger spacecraft that looks like two soda cans, one stacked on top of the other, essentially two MX-1Es. One is almost the same as the lander on the first mission. The second module — without landing legs — is a propulsion stage that would enable the spacecraft to reach the moon's south pole, where ice persists inside craters that are eternally in shadows.

Ice is a valuable resource for future human settlements, beyond providing water to drink. Water molecules broken up into hydrogen and oxygen could not only provide air for astronauts to breathe, but also rocket propellent. The ice at the bottom of the craters probably preserves molecules from the earliest days of the solar system, too, which could be a boon for scientists.

That same configuration, called MX-2, could also be sent as far away as the moons of Mars, but to land on Mars would require a more complex, more expensive vehicle beyond Moon Express's current designs. "It can get basically anywhere in the inner solar system," Dr. Richards said, meaning the neighborhood from the sun to Mars.

Two additional configurations would put together multiple building block propulsion modules in larger moon landers. A propulsion module at the center could serve as a smaller vehicle that could blast off from the moon, bringing back rocks and soil samples to Earth.

The cost of building and launching a MX-1E is less than $10 million, Dr. Richards said. NASA missions, by comparison, typically cost hundreds of millions of dollars.

"We want to collapse the cost of getting to the moon and by doing so, there is going to be a brand new market that is going to emerge," Dr. Richards said.

He said he hoped that in the years to come, Moon Express would be launching at least twice a year.

Moon Express is not the only company betting on the moon, which has been largely overlooked since the end of NASA's Apollo missions four decades ago.

The Google Lunar X Prize was intended to spur commercial endeavors, but the pace of progress has been slower and harder than organizers anticipated with the deadline extended twice. There will be no more extensions, X Prize officials have said.

Astrobotic Technology of Pittsburgh dropped out of the competition last year because the 2017 deadline proved unrealistic. It is still developing its Peregrine lander and now plans a 2019 launch, with 11 customers signed up.

"We're happy with where we're at," said John Thornton, Astrobotic's chief executive. He said Astrobotic was aiming to launch once every two years and then increase the rate to once a year.

Blue Origin, the rocket company created by Jeffrey P. Bezos, founder, chairman and chief executive of Amazon, has also expressed interest in traveling to the moon, proposing a large robotic spacecraft called Blue Moon to ship supplies for a future human settlement there.

Elon Musk's Mars Vision: A One-Size-Fits-All Rocket. A Very Big One.

BY ADAM BAIDAWI AND KENNETH CHANG | SEPT. 28, 2017

ADELAIDE, AUSTRALIA — Elon Musk is revising his ambitions for sending people to Mars, and he says he now has a clearer picture of how his company, SpaceX, can make money along the way.

The key is a new rocket — smaller than the one he described at a conference in Mexico last year but still bigger than anything ever launched — and a new spaceship.

Speaking on Friday at the International Astronautical Congress in Adelaide, Australia, Mr. Musk said he had figured out a workable business plan, although his presentation lacked financial figures to back up his assertions.

Mr. Musk has long talked about his dreams of colonizing Mars, and at the same conference last year, he finally provided engineering details: a humongous reusable rocket called the Interplanetary Transport System.

But he did not convincingly explain then how SpaceX, still a company of modest size and revenues, could finance such an ambitious project.

"Now we think we have a better way to do it," he said Friday.

The new rocket and spaceship would replace everything that SpaceX is currently launching or plans to launch in the near future. "That's really fundamental," Mr. Musk said.

The slimmed-down rocket would be nine meters, or about 30 feet, in diameter instead of the 12-meter behemoth he described last year. It would still be more powerful than the Saturn 5 rocket that took NASA astronauts to the moon. Mr. Musk called it B.F.R. (The "B" stands for "big"; the "R" is for "rocket.") The B.F.R. would be able to lift 150 metric tons to low-Earth orbit, Mr. Musk said.

For Mars colonists, the rocket would lift a spaceship with 40 cabins, and with two to three people per cabin, it would carry about 100 people per flight. After launching, the B.F.R. booster would return to the launching pad; the spaceship would continue to orbit, where it would refill its tanks of methane and oxygen propellant before embarking on the monthslong journey to Mars.

But with the smaller size, the B.F.R. would also be useful much closer to Earth, Mr. Musk said. He said it would be able to take over the launching duties of SpaceX's current Falcon 9 rocket, taking many satellites to orbit at once, as well as ferry cargo and astronauts to the International Space Station. A variation of the spaceship could be used to collect and dispose of relics of satellite and other debris cluttering low-Earth orbit, he said.

Because all parts of the rocket and the spaceship are to be fully reusable, the cost of operating them would be low.

Robert Zubrin, president of the Mars Society, a nonprofit organization that advocates human exploration and settlement of the planet, liked the changes that Mr. Musk has made. "This is a much more practical approach than he presented last year," Dr. Zubrin said. "It means he is serious."

The same spaceship could also land on the moon. "It's 2017," Mr. Musk said. "We should have a lunar base by now."

Even on Earth, the rockets, traveling at up to 18,000 miles per hour, could make long-distance trips short — New York to Shanghai in 39 minutes, for example. Any two points on Earth would be less than an hour apart, Mr. Musk said.

After the presentation, Mr. Musk took to Instagram to elaborate on the price of those round-the-world rocket flights: "Cost per seat should be about the same as full fare economy in an aircraft. Forgot to mention that."

Mr. Musk maintained a highly optimistic schedule for his Mars dreams. He said the company had already started work to build pieces of the new rocket.

A cargo mission, without any passengers, could launch as early as 2022. "That's not a typo, although it is aspirational," he said. "Five years feels like a long time to me."

Two years later, the next time that Mars and Earth would swing by each other, SpaceX would launch four B.F.R.s to Mars — two carrying cargo, two carrying people.

In the lead-up to Mr. Musk's talk on Friday, the main entrance to the Adelaide Convention Center was closed and locked, with a swell of people outside waiting to get in.

"He's such an iconic character," said Paris Michaels, the chief executive of Air@Wave Communications in Sydney, who attended the congress. "I planned the day around making this event. I'm taking a later flight home, even though I'm averaging two hours' sleep this week."

SpaceX is not the only company with proposals for the Red Planet. A few hours before Mr. Musk's talk on Friday, Lockheed Martin provided an update of its own Mars mission vision, called Mars Base Camp. Compared with Mr. Musk's ambitions, the Lockheed Martin plan seems quaint and slow. It would not head to Mars until 2028, it would take only six astronauts, and the first trip would not even land on Mars but instead circle the planet for a year before returning to Earth.

From Mars orbit, astronauts could control robotic explorers like rovers and flying drones.

Mars Base Camp is more of a suggestion to NASA of what the agency could do rather than a corporate strategy that Lockheed Martin would pursue by itself.

"This isn't Lockheed Martin's vision, and it's not the only vision of how to get to Mars, but we put it out here so that we can globally begin the dialogue," Robert Chambers, an engineer working on the Mars Base Camp concept, said during the presentation.

Unlike Mr. Musk's dreams, Mars Base Camp would not require unproven business plans or novel technologies far beyond what already exists or is already in development. "We know how to do this," Mr. Chambers said.

The spacecraft, which looks as one might expect a traditional NASA expeditionary mission to Mars to look, would incorporate both the Orion crew capsule that Lockheed Martin is building for NASA deep-space missions and the agency's plans to put a space station high above the moon. This week, the Russian space agency announced that it would like to collaborate with NASA on this lunar space station, called the Deep Space Gateway.

Lockheed Martin is one of six companies that NASA selected to develop a prototype of a habitat module that could be used for the Deep Space Gateway. Lockheed Martin officials said their vision for Mars Base Camp did not depend on their design's being selected.

The Mars Base Camp proposal would also fit within the NASA budget, Lockheed Martin officials said.

This year's update unveiled a reusable, hydrogen-fueled lander that would take astronauts to the Martian surface on a follow-up mission. Up to four astronauts could live on the Martian surface for two weeks at a time in the lander.

Reflecting the interest of many to return to the moon before going to Mars, Lockheed Martin officials said the lander could also be used to travel to different parts of the moon from the Deep Space Gateway.

In This Space Race, Jeff Bezos and Elon Musk Are Competing to Take You There

BY WALTER ISAACSON | APRIL 24, 2018

THE SPACE BARONS: Elon Musk, Jeff Bezos, and the Quest to Colonize the Cosmos. By Christian Davenport. Illustrated. 308 pp. PublicAffairs. $28.

ROCKET BILLIONAIRES: Elon Musk, Jeff Bezos, and the New Space Race. By Tim Fernholz. Illustrated. 281 pp. Houghton Mifflin Harcourt. $28.

LAUNCH PAD 39A, just north of Cape Canaveral, Fla., was the storied site where America's space dreams and the imaginations of its youth were sent soaring. The first manned mission to the moon blasted off from there in 1969, as did the last, in 1972; so did the first space shuttle mission, in 1981, and the last, in 2011. But by 2013, with the shuttle program grounded and America's half century of space aspirations having ended with bangs and whimpers, 39A was rusting away and weeds were growing through its flame trench. A crippled NASA was eager to sell it.

The space agency knew there was a natural customer: Elon Musk, the cheeky PayPal co-founder and Tesla creator whose SpaceX venture had become the first private rocket company to launch into orbit with a payload. Musk's mesmerizing style — skittering on the border between visionary and eccentric — made it seem at times that his obsession with space travel involved a desire to return to some celestial home, but his Falcon rockets had won NASA's respect. Surprisingly, a second bidder emerged: Amazon's Jeff Bezos, who pursued his passion for all things, including space travel, with an awesome talent for being both exuberant and methodical. His company, Blue Origin, was building a reusable launch vehicle that, among other things, planned to take tourists into space.

Musk won the bidding for Launch Pad 39A, but a few months later Bezos bought the nearby Launch Complex 36, from which missions to fly by Mars and Venus had been launched. The transfer of these hallowed pads represented, both symbolically and in practice, John F. Kennedy's torch of space exploration being passed from government to the private sector — from a once-glorious but now sclerotic federal agency to a new breed of boyish billionaires who embodied the daring passion and imagination of history's great pioneers, adventurers and innovators.

Two new books chronicle this fascinating transition. "The Space Barons," by Christian Davenport, a Washington Post reporter, is an exciting narrative filled with colorful reporting and sharp insights. The book sparkles because of Davenport's access to the main players and his talent for crisp storytelling. "Rocket Billionaires," by Tim Fernholz, a reporter for Quartz, is not quite as vibrant a narrative and lacks some of Davenport's memorable scenes, but it provides smart analysis of the New Space sector as well as historical context about NASA's triumphs and failures.

In the class that I teach on the history of the digital revolution, the students discuss whether innovation is driven more by big government projects or by nimble entrepreneurs. The answer, of course, is that it usually involves a symbiotic mix, like the semiconductor industry, which arose out of the Pentagon and NASA's need to put guidance systems in the nose cones of rockets. Vannevar Bush was the dean of engineering at the Massachusetts Institute of Technology, a co-founder of Raytheon, and oversaw the government science programs that resulted in the atom bomb and electronic computer. He wrote a seminal paper in 1945, called "Science — the Endless Frontier," which described how a collaboration of all three sectors he had been part of — academia, business and government — would drive innovation. Government funding of basic research in university labs would lead to discoveries in fundamental science that would be the "seed" for future inventions.

Many innovations have progressed along that path. The ENIAC computer funded by the United States Army and built at the University of Pennsylvania was the genesis for UNIVAC and then most other electronic computers. The network funded by the Defense Advanced Research Projects Agency and designed by a consortium of academic and private labs led eventually to today's internet. The National Science Foundation, started based on Vannevar Bush's paper, created a multiagency Digital Library Initiative that funded the academic research of Larry Page and Sergey Brin, which led to Google. The sequencing of the human genome, largely funded by the National Institutes of Health, planted the seeds for the biotech industry.

Now space endeavors are following this "innovation progression," as we can call it. "Just as Darpa served as the initial impetus for the internet and underwrote a lot of the costs of developing the internet in the beginning, it may be the case that NASA has essentially done the same thing by spending the money to build sort of fundamental technologies," Musk said a year after launching SpaceX. "Once we can bring the sort of commercial, free enterprise sector into it, then we can see the dramatic acceleration that we saw in the internet."

One of the first private pioneers was Burt Rutan, a mutton-chopped aircraft designer who regarded NASA as a bloated and unimaginative bureaucracy and in 1982 founded a company called Scaled Composites that designed aircraft so innovative that, as Davenport writes, "it was as if his inspiration came not just from the laws of aerodynamics but from Picasso." One of his ideas was for a manned aircraft that could reach the edge of space and then fold its wings upward to act as a feather allowing the craft to re-enter the earth's atmosphere, land on a runway, and be reused. It would become his entry in the Ansari X Prize, which offered $10 million for the first private company that could launch a reusable vehicle to space twice within two weeks.

Rutan attracted two billionaire partners. The first was the Microsoft co-founder Paul Allen, who as a schoolboy in Seattle yearned to become an astronaut but, being nearsighted, realized that was impossible so spent his time coding in the school's computer room with his friend Bill Gates. Rutan's second partner was the toothy goldilocked Richard Branson, a thrill-addicted serial adventurer and entrepreneur who was as enthusiastic about publicity as Allen was averse to it. Branson's personal motto for his company, Virgin, was "Screw it, let's do it," which was no longer a guiding principle at NASA, and he created Virgin Galactic with the goal of taking tourists into space. "Paul, isn't this better than the best sex you ever had?" Branson asked Allen during one test flight as the spaceship climbed higher.

In 2004, Rutan's craft (with a Virgin logo on its tail) flew twice to space and back to win the X Prize. At the celebration, Rutan took a shot at NASA. "I was thinking a little bit about that other space agency, the big guys," he said. "I think they're looking at each other now and saying, 'We're screwed.' " Branson began selling tickets at prices that started at $200,000 to those who wanted to ride in a similar plane he began building, the launch date of which always seems to be about a year away.

Elon Musk's love of adventure came partly from his maternal grandfather, an accomplished amateur pilot in South Africa who in 1952 completed a 22,000-mile journey across the globe with no electronic instruments. Musk founded SpaceX in 2002 with the eventual goal of colonizing Mars. "The more Musk studied, the more he realized that there had been very little advancement in rocket technology in the past 40 years," Davenport writes. "To a self-made Silicon Valley tech entrepreneur, this was stunning." His company's mantra was, "Set audacious, nearly impossible goals and don't get dissuaded."

Musk's entrepreneurship had a social purpose. SpaceX, Tesla, his electric car company, and SolarCity, his renewable energy company, Fernholz writes, "were explicitly intended to further human civilization." Along the way, he developed a cultlike following. When SpaceX managed to launch a space capsule into orbit and dock it at the International Space Station in 2012, something NASA could no longer do on its own, the employees at his headquarters broke into a chant, "We love Elon!"

Bezos was likewise inspired by his own maternal grandfather. Lawrence Preston Gise, an upright but loving naval commander, helped develop the hydrogen bomb during a stint at the Atomic Energy Commission and then retired to his sprawling Texas ranch to enjoy his family — and in particular his insatiably curious little grandson with very big ears, smile and laugh. Bezos' passion for space began when he was 5 and he watched with his family the launch of Apollo 11, the manned moon mission commanded by Neil Armstrong. "It really was a seminal moment for me," he said. "I remember watching it on our living room TV, and the excitement of my parents and my grandparents. Little kids can pick up that kind of excitement."

Bezos spent every summer at his grandfather's ranch, where he fixed windmills, castrated cattle and geeked out on the tiny county library's surprisingly large sci-fi collection. His high school valedictorian speech was about space: how to colonize planets, build space hotels and save our fragile planet. "Space, the final frontier, meet me there!" he concluded.

When Bezos founded Blue Origin in 2000, naming it after that pale blue planet where humans originated, he called upon one of his favorite science fiction writers, Neal Stephenson, to be an adviser. They kicked around wildly novel ideas, such as using a bullwhip-like device to propel objects into space. Eventually Bezos focused on reusable rockets. "How is the situation in the year 2000 different from 1960?" Stephenson asked him. "What's different is computer sensors, cameras, software. Being able to land vertically is the kind of problem that can be addressed by those technologies that existed in 2000 that didn't exist in 1960."

Bezos began putting together a huge tract of ranch land in Texas where he could build his reusable rockets in secret. One of the great scenes in Davenport's book is the description of the helicopter trip Bezos took to find the land, which ended with a terrifying crash. He survived, and it conditioned him to the fact that flying machines sometimes fail. Among Bezos' many strengths is to be exuberant patiently, to have a long-term horizon, as he has done at Amazon. At his Texas ranch, he has begun construction of a 10,000-year "Clock of the Long Now" designed by the futurist Danny Hillis, which has a century hand that advances every hundred years and a cuckoo that comes out every millennium. In the mission statement for his space company, he wrote, "Blue will pursue this long-term objective patiently, step by step." As Elon Musk pushed forward with very public fits and starts, Bezos advised his team, "Be the tortoise and not the hare."

At the end of 2015, within a month of each other, Musk and Bezos both launched rockets that returned safely to earth and were reusable. For the moment, Musk the hare had darted ahead: His powerful Falcon 9 rocket had lifted a payload into orbit, whereas Bezos' smaller New Shepard craft had merely gone up into the edge of space and returned. But as happens with scrappy entrepreneurial business competitors, in contrast to government bureaucracies, Bezos and Musk were goading each other on. And unlike the race between the tortoise and the hare, they can both triumph — as can, one hopes, Richard Branson and others.

Indeed, even NASA and its big corporate contractor, the United Launch Alliance, a venture between Lockheed Martin and Boeing, can come out winners from competition. As is often the case with the innovation progression, the greatest technological advances come when a symbiosis is reached that combines the resources of a visionary government and the scrappiness of risk-taking entrepreneurs, each spurring the other onward and upward.

WALTER ISAACSON is a professor of history at Tulane. His books include "The Innovators" and biographies of Benjamin Franklin, Albert Einstein, Steve Jobs and Leonardo da Vinci.

The Rich Are Planning to Leave This Wretched Planet

BY SHEILA MARIKAR | JUNE 9, 2018

Here comes private space travel — with cocktails, retro-futuristic Philippe Starck designs and Wi-Fi. Just $55 million a trip!

HOUSTON — In an era in which privileged individuals search constantly for the next experience to obsess over and post about on social media, space truly remains the final frontier, a luxury that only the one percent of the one percent can afford. Brad Pitt and Katy Perry are among those who have reportedly plunked down $250,000 for a ride on one of Richard Branson's Virgin Galactic spaceships, undaunted by a 2014 test flight that crashed and killed one pilot. Now a company called Axiom Space is giving those with piles of money and an adventuresome spirit something new to lust after: the prospect of an eight-day trip to space that is plush, if not entirely comfortable, and with a bit of the luster of NASA as well.

Circumambulating the floor of his gray carpeted office on a recent Wednesday, Mike Suffredini — NASA veteran, Houston native and the chief executive officer of Axiom Space — stopped in front of a wood compartment about as big as a telephone booth.

"It's no New York hotel room," he said with a shrug, as if apologizing for its size.

"It pretty much is, actually!" said Gabrielle Rein, Axiom's marketing director.

"It" was an early mock-up of a cabin that will reside inside a commercial space station, among the first of its kind, that Axiom is building: a mash-up of boutique hotel, adult space camp, and NASA-grade research facility designed to hover approximately 250 miles above the earth. Axiom hired Philippe Starck, the French designer who has lent panache to everything from high-end hotel rooms to mass-market baby monitors, to outfit the interior of its cabins. Mr. Starck lined the walls with a padded, quilted, cream-colored, suede-like fabric and hundreds of tiny LED lights that glow in varying hues depending on the time of day and where the space station is floating in relation to the earth.

"My vision is to create a comfortable egg, friendly, where walls are so soft and in harmony with the movements of the human body in zero gravity," Mr. Starck wrote in an email, calling his intended effect "a first approach to infinity. The traveler should physically and mentally feel his or her action of floating in the universe."

Brace for the rise of the cosmos-scenti.

At NASA, Mr. Suffredini spent a decade managing the International Space Station, the hulking, 20-year-old research facility in low Earth orbit. This gives him a certain edge over Mr. Branson and Jeff Bezos, the founder of Amazon, who is overseeing Blue Origin. (The majority of Axiom's 60 employees also hail from NASA.) At least Mr. Suffredini thinks so.

"The guys who are doing Blue Origin, and Virgin Galactic are going to the edge of space — they're not going into orbit," he said. "What they're doing is a cool experience. It gives you about 15 minutes of microgravity and you see the curvature of the earth, but you don't get the same experience that you get from viewing the earth from above, and spending time reflecting, contemplating."

And, naturally, posting to Instagram.

"There will be Wi-Fi," Mr. Suffredini said. "Everybody will be online. They can make phone calls, sleep, look out the window."

Maybe it will be so nice they'll want to stay there.

But the Cost! And the Claustrophobia!

The Starck-designed station will supposedly open in 2022, but Axiom says they can start sending curious travelers into orbit as early as 2020. (Note: nearly everything space-related is delayed by years, sometimes decades.) They'll just have to make do with the comparatively rugged accommodations of the International Space Station, which is working with Axiom in addition to other commercial space station outfits.

Axiom's station can house eight passengers, including a professional astronaut. Each will pay $55 million for the adventure, which includes 15 weeks of training, much of it at the Johnson Space Center, a 10-minute drive from Axiom's headquarters, and possibly a trip on one of Elon Musk's SpaceX rockets. Thus far, three entities have signed up for on-the-ground training, which starts at $1 million, Mr. Suffredini said, though he declined to name them. The inaugural trip will be only $50 million. "It's a bargain!" he said.

"The lion's share of the cost comes from the flight up and down," Mr. Suffredini went on. "Rocket rides are expensive. You know people" — meaning competitors — "don't know what they're talking about if they're quoting prices substantially less than what we're stating."

In the land rush to space, as it were, Aurora Station, a luxury space hotel being built by Orion Span, another Houston-based aerospace company, announced in April that it would charge $9.5 million per passenger for a 12-day trip, but did not mention the cost of the rocket ride there and back. (Meanwhile, NanoRacks says they'll build space "outposts" from spent rocket stages and will create "near space" habitats, including for tourism, and Bigelow Aerospace says they're putting big inflatable space pods into orbit, though tourism isn't their focus.)

Phil Larson, a former space policy adviser to President Barack Obama who also worked for SpaceX, doesn't expect travel prices to drop dramatically in the next few years. "These habitat and outpost companies are great, but we need to solve the launch cost and transportation problem," said Mr. Larson. "It's like the biggest elephant in the room nobody talks about."

The barriers to entry, beyond cost? Being 21 or older — there's no age cap — and passing a medical exam, administered before the rest of training begins, as well as "The Right Stuff"-like tests of mind and mettle, like a spin in a human centrifuge (even the YouTube videos are hard to stomach). "Not only do you experience the Gs, you get put into a can that's really — I mean, if you're going to be a little claustrophobic, this is where you're going to feel it," said Mr. Suffredini. "About half the people that fly get sick for the first two or three days. Going with us for eight days gives you a chance to get over that. If you don't get sick, you have all this time!"

Axiom guests will be required to wear a NASA-grade spacesuit for the rocket ride to and from the station. (Features include a fiberglass torso and a drink tube for consuming small sips of water. Also, a diaper.) Years after Pierre Cardin, Paco Rabanne and Andre Courrèges envisioned space-age fashion, Axiom is also in talks with a high-end European fashion house it also declined to name about custom-designing leisure suits travelers can wear once they dock. "They will be tailored to each person and can be customized with their own logo, if they want," Ms. Rein said "It's a very special keepsake and part of their luxury experience."

GLAMPING AT 1,320,000 FEET

To understand the grand scale of Axiom's plans, it helps to know that astronauts have, thus far, largely been roughing it up there. The Johnson Space Center contains a life-size mock-up of the ISS, whose drab, beige interior is lined with drab, gray handholds to tether down things and people, necessary given the lack of gravity. A tour guide quaintly referred to the onboard bathroom as a "potty." There are no showers.

"The few folks that have gone to orbit as tourists, it wasn't really a luxurious experience, it was kind of like camping," said Mr. Suffredini. The Axiom station will still have hand holds, but thanks to Mr. Starck (who Mr. Suffredini hadn't heard of before Axiom's branding consultant suggested they hire him) they will be plated in gold or wrapped in buttery leather, like the steering wheel of a Mercedes. Axiom's private cabins will have screens for Netflixing and chilling — there's not a lot to do up there, although going outside to do a spacewalk is a possibility — and there will be a great, glass-walled cupola to gather with travelers and take in a more panoramic view of the earth, perhaps with an adult beverage.

"Wine and cocktails work well," said Michael Baine, Axiom's chief engineer. "Beer and carbonated beverages do not. You don't have the gravity to separate the carbon dioxide in your stomach so it causes a lot of bloating." (Shades of the Fizzy-Lifting Drink scene in "Charlie and the Chocolate Factory.")

You'll want to pack deodorant. "There's a hygiene compartment where you do kind of a sponge bath," said Mr. Suffredini.

Fond of folksy sayings (he referred to wine as "fruit of the vine") and thorough explanations, Mr. Suffredini, who is 59, retired from NASA in 2015 with the intent of starting a commercial space venture. Soon after leaving, he became the president of the commercial space division of the engineering firm Stinger Ghaffarian Technologies, and in 2016, launched Axiom, which has raised more than $10 million in funding so far.

"We've met their engineers, we've seen their plans, we hired domain experts that grilled them and did a deeper dive," said Lisa Rich, a founder of Hemisphere Ventures and an early Axiom investor. "Everything came up with 'This is a big go sign, we've got to get in on this.' "

"At the Johnson Space Center, when Mike walks down the hall, they're all practically saluting him," Ms. Rich said. "He's a legend in his own right."

Mr. Suffredini's professional life has revolved around space. "I was like everybody who watched Neil Armstrong walk on the moon and decided that NASA was cool and wanted to work there," he said. But while he's overseen many missions, he hasn't been in orbit and has no plans to see Axiom for himself. ("We'd have to work out who's going to cover my cost," he demurred, when asked.)

Still, Mr. Suffredini sees Axiom as a necessary step in continuing scientific research and development in space, which he believes is crucial to the survival of our species. His company may cater to rich thrill seekers, but he insists he is an idealist.

"If you just go visit and come back, you're not pioneering," he said. "You've got to pioneer."

Pioneers include countries who have yet to send someone to space (a German organization seeking to get that country's first female astronaut in orbit is in talks with Axiom), material-science researchers, and biologists trying to understand how the human body adapts outside earth's atmosphere. Also, maybe, Tupperware.

"They're interested in working with us," Mr. Suffredini said, "testing different types of containers, seeing how you can cook in them in a sort of clean way. But with this idea, this grand idea that we have, comes cleaning dishes and cleaning a microwave, and who wants to do that? Pretty soon we're going to be flying a butler with every crew."

Meet SpaceX's First Moon Voyage Customer, Yusaku Maezawa

BY KENNETH CHANG | SEPT. 17, 2018

ELON MUSK on Monday evening introduced Yusaku Maezawa, founder of the online Japanese clothing company Zozo, as his first customer for a voyage around the moon aboard a SpaceX rocket.

"Finally, I can tell you that I choose to go the moon," Mr. Maezawa shouted.

Mr. Maezawa's intent to follow in the contrails of American astronauts, who first looped the moon in 1968 aboard the Apollo 8 mission, was announced at an event at the company's headquarters in the Los Angeles area. The expensive trip would cost at least tens of millions of dollars, if not a couple of hundred million, and when it would occur was not yet announced. Neither Mr. Musk nor Mr. Maezawa would disclose the price.

Mr. Maezawa is to ride a yet-to-be-built rocket known as the B.F.R. on a journey that would take four to five days. The rocket would not be ready for the trip until 2023, Mr. Musk said, and would cost from $2 billion to $10 billion to develop. He added that Mr. Maezawa's ticket would make a meaningful contribution to the project's completion.

While SpaceX's technological achievements are significant, Mr. Musk's forecasts of SpaceX's timelines have usually turned out to be far too optimistic.

Development of the Falcon Heavy rocket, for example, which finally made a maiden test flight in February, took more than four years longer than Mr. Musk had anticipated. And his earlier announcements had suggested that the B.F.R. would be ready for an uncrewed trip to Mars as soon as 2022.

This summer has been a tumultuous time for Mr. Musk and another of his companies, the electric carmaker Tesla. On Twitter, Mr. Musk announced a plan to take the publicly traded car company private, then changed his mind three weeks later. Tesla has been struggling to meet production targets of its Model 3 sedan, and Mr. Musk said he had sometimes slept at the factory.

He also enlisted his engineers to build a submarine-like escape pod to rescue 12 boys and their coach from a cave in Thailand. That proved unnecessary — the boys were able to swim out with the help of divers.

But when one of the divers, Vernon Unsworth, disparaged the effort, Mr. Musk suggested, without evidence, that Mr. Unsworth was a pedophile. On Monday, Mr. Unsworth announced that he was suing Mr. Musk for defamation.

By comparison, SpaceX has been an oasis of calm, launching satellites and spacecraft without incident for most of the year.

Mr. Maezawa, a billionaire fashion entrepreneur, may be best known in the United States for his purchase in 2017 of a 1982 painting by Jean-Michel Basquiat for $110 million. The artist's sister, Lisane Basquiat, said in an interview at the time that "we were speechless" about the price he paid.

Mr. Maezawa said he'd like to bring five to eight artists aboard the trip, part of a project he called Dear Moon.

This is actually the second time that SpaceX has announced that it will fly tourists to the moon and back.

In February last year, Mr. Musk said that two people had put down a deposit for a cruise around the moon and that it would occur in late 2018. However, those two were to fly aboard the Falcon Heavy. Mr. Musk said on Monday that Mr. Maezawa — and an invited fellow passenger — had been his customer for that trip.

With the modernization of electronics leading to smaller satellites and the greater lifting power of newer versions of SpaceX's workhorse Falcon 9 rocket, the market for the Falcon Heavy is dwindling. (The Heavy has yet to make a second flight, although SpaceX lists the United States Air Force and satellite companies as future customers.) Mr. Musk said in February that SpaceX would not go to the expense and effort of making the Falcon Heavy suitable for human passengers.

Elon Musk, left, the chief executive of SpaceX, introduced Yusaku Maezawa, the founder of the online fashion retailer Zozo, on Monday as the first customer for a trip around the moon with one of the company's rockets.

At the same time, SpaceX has begun work on the B.F.R., its next-generation behemoth rocket, more powerful than the Saturn 5 that NASA used for the Apollo missions. The rocket is intended to replace both the Falcon 9 and the Falcon Heavy and is ultimately designed to take 100 people on a journey to Mars. (The "B" stands for "big;" the "R" is for "rocket." In public, Gwynne Shotwell, SpaceX's president, states its full name as "Big Falcon Rocket." Mr. Musk and the company's news releases have remained ambiguous about what the "F" stands for.)

Even if the Falcon Heavy had been ready for the moon tourists, development of the SpaceX capsule for taking astronauts to space, which would have been required for a Falcon Heavy trip, has also been delayed. The first flight of that spacecraft ferrying NASA astronauts to the International Space Station is now scheduled for next year, and watchdog agencies within the government say further delays are possible.

Since the retirement of the space shuttles in 2011, NASA has been relying on Russia to carry its astronauts to and from the International Space Station, but that contract ends in November 2019.

The B.F.R. is far more ambitious than the Falcon 9 and the Falcon Heavy — larger, more powerful and fully reusable — and thus even more likely to encounter technological snags, and the design of the B.F.R. is still evolving.

Two years ago, Mr. Musk described a gigantic, 40-foot-diameter rocket, then known as the Interplanetary Transport, before unveiling a slimmed-down B.F.R., which is only 30 feet wide. The images released in recent days by SpaceX show larger fins on the B.F.R. than what had been seen previously, giving it an appearance more reminiscent of NASA's retired space shuttles. At the news conference on Monday, Mr. Musk said it was an iteration of the earlier design.

So far, seven people have paid for a trip to space, riding on a Russian Soyuz rocket for short stays at the International Space Station. (One person, Charles Simonyi, has made two trips.)

No tourists have gone to orbit since 2009. Other companies, including Virgin Galactic and Blue Origin, are looking to start selling suborbital trips — rides that cross the boundary into outer space — before coming right back down, offering a few minutes of weightlessness.

CHAPTER 4

New Views of the Solar System

The rising enthusiasm for exoplanets and private space-flight has rippled across the world. Asteroid Oumuamua, passing through from a distant solar system, caused a flurry of research and speculation. Probe flybys of Jupiter's and Saturn's moons left suggestions of microbial life there, while Venus and our own moon offered new clues to the formation of planets. As technological advances facilitate new exploration, some of the benefits will include further research in our celestial backyard.

The Moon Comes Around Again

BY NATALIE ANGIER | SEPT. 7, 2014

AS THE MOON wheels around Earth every 28 days and shows us a progressively greater and then stingier slice of its sun-lightened face, the distance between moon and Earth changes, too. At the nearest point along its egg-shaped orbit, its perigee, the moon may be 26,000 miles closer to us than it is at its far point.

And should the moon happen to hit its ever-shifting orbital perigee at the same time that it lies athwart from the sun, we are treated to a so-called supermoon, a full moon that can seem embraceably close — as much as 12 percent bigger and 30 percent brighter than the average full moon.

If the weather is good where you are, please, go out Monday or Tuesday night and gawk for yourself: A supermoon will be dominating the sky. It's the last of this summer's impressive run of three super-moons, and the final one of the year.

Some astronomers dislike the whole supermoon hoopla. They point out that the term originated with astrology, not astronomy; that peri-gee full moons are not all that rare, coming an average of every 13 ½ months; and that their apparently swollen dimensions are often as much a matter of optical illusion and wishful blinking as of relative lunar nearness. The superstar astronomer Neil deGrasse Tyson grumbled archly on Twitter that the "perennially hyped" term debases the legacy of Superman, supernovas and the video game character Super Mario.

Still, astronomers concur that whatever the reason, yes, you should look at the moon early and often, whether it's waxing or waning, gib-bous or crescent, and appreciate the many features that set our moon apart from the other 100-plus moons of the solar system, and even cel-ebrate our loyal satellite as a planet in its own right.

"I know it goes contrary to the nomenclature currently used," said David A. Paige, a professor of planetary science at the University of California, Los Angeles, referring to the definition of a planet as the dominant gravitational object in its orbit. "But where I come from, anything that's big enough to be round is a planet." Unlike most moons of the solar system, ours has the heft to pull itself into a sphere.

SPARKS OF DISCOVERY

Scientists say that while the public may think of the moon as a problem solved and a bit retro — the place astronauts visited a half-dozen times way back before Watergate and then abandoned with a giant "meh" from mankind — in fact, lunar studies is a vibrant enterprise that is yielding a wealth of insights and surprises.

One research group reported new evidence that the moon was born violently, in an act of planetary suicide that left faint but read-able fingerprints. Another team proposed that the moon's cataclys-mic origins could explain the mysterious lunar features we know as the man in the moon.

This 1967 photograph was made by NASA's Lunar Orbiter 4. The impact basin seen here is called Mare Orientale, and is located on the Moon's extreme western edge. It's difficult to see from an earthbound perspective, and is over 3 billion years old.

Partly on the basis of data from NASA's Lunar Reconnaissance Orbiter, a multi-instrument spacecraft that has been orbiting, mapping and analyzing the moon since 2009, researchers have found that the moon is a place of thermal lunacy, of searing heat crossed with sub-Plutonic cold, and of pockets that may be the most frigid spots in the entire solar system. Recent measurements taken inside impact craters at the lunar poles, where no solar light is thought to have penetrated for a billion years or more, showed temperatures of about 30 degrees Celsius above absolute zero, Dr. Paige said.

Andrew Jordan of the University of New Hampshire and his colleagues have calculated that these temperature extremes could give rise to a novel form of sparkiness, tiny bolts of lightning that dance silently through the moon's airless landscape and fluff up the soil as they flash.

Reporting in The Journal of Geophysical Research: Planets, the researchers proposed that charged particles from the sun could be getting trapped at slightly different depths of the frigid lunar surface, forming electric fields. Those fields would gradually build up strength until, zap, serious sparks start to fly, which in turn would vaporize particles of soil.

Sparking events, the researchers said, could explain the foamy appearance of soil recently detected by NASA's orbiter. The lunar surface "may be far more active than we thought," Dr. Jordan said. "It's amazing to have this kind of natural laboratory almost in our spatial backyard."

At an average distance of 238,855 miles, the moon is indeed on Earth's patio: string together just 11 round trips from New York to Tasmania, and you're there. The moon is not the largest satellite in the solar system — three moons of Jupiter and one of Saturn are bigger — but with a diameter almost 30 percent of Earth's, it is by far the largest relative to its planet. Jupiter's Ganymede, for example, which tops the lunar size chart, measures just 4 percent the diameter of its gas-giant sponsor.

A VIOLENT BIRTH

Another outstanding feature of the moon is its origin. Most of the other moons in the solar system are thought to be celestial passers-by that were pulled into a planet's orbit, or to have formed contemporaneously with their planet from an initial starter disc of dust, gas and rock. The moon, by contrast, is thought to have a bloodier past.

According to the reigning hypothesis, about 4.5 billion years ago, shortly after Earth had accreted down into a sphere from its little slub of circumsolar material, another newborn planet, still shaky on its feet, slammed obliquely into Earth with terrifying force.

That "giant impactor," Theia, who in Greek mythology was mother to the goddess of the moon, is thought to have been roughly the size of Mars and to have been pulverized in the encounter, along with a good chunk of proto-Earth. From that fiery cloud of all-Theia and part-Earth, the scenario goes, our moon soon condensed.

The impactor hypothesis made sense and comported with computer models, but hard evidence for it proved elusive. If the moon was partly the offspring of a non-Earth body — Theia — there should be chemical fingerprints attesting to the foreign parentage. Astronomers who have analyzed a wide array of extraterrestrial material have determined that the many residents of the solar system differ measurably in their isotope ratios, the forms of the chemical elements they carry. (Heavy oxygen or light? Titanium with more neutrons or fewer?) But when researchers checked the isotope content in rocks from the moon, the ratios looked identical to rocks on Earth. Where were the traces of Theia?

Now it looks as if the evidence has arrived. This summer, Daniel Herwartz, a geochemist working at the University of Göttingen in Germany and his colleagues reported in the journal Science that they had detected isotopic ratios of oxygen in lunar rocks that were unlike the forms of oxygen found on Earth. It is, Dr. Herwartz said, "the difference between Earth and moon predicted by the impact theory."

The researchers stumbled to victory accidentally, he said. As geochemists, they had developed new techniques for more precisely measuring oxygen isotopes to address Earth-based geological problems. "When that succeeded," Dr. Herwartz said, "we thought we'd have a look at the moon question again."

Initial efforts foundered. "NASA doesn't hand out Apollo samples to everybody," he said, referring to rocks brought back decades ago by astronauts. So the scientists tried to work with meteorite fragments, which proved too disturbed to be useful.

They then persuaded the space agency to hand over a baby aspirin's worth of pure Apollo rock, and, sure enough, there was Theia's isotopic thumbprint.

EMERGING FROM THE DARKNESS

Other signs of the fiery collision may linger in the moon's familiar patchwork of dark and light splotches that has long been likened, dubiously, to a man's face. It's the only side of the moon we ever see from home base, a result of Earth's having yanked its satellite into a so-called tidal lock: The time it takes the moon to rotate once on its axis is the same as the four weeks it takes to orbit Earth, which means the same side is always turned toward us.

"It's the minimum energy configuration, the most stable configuration the two can take," said Arpita Roy, a doctoral student in astronomy and astrophysics at Penn State who is also an author of a new report in The Astrophysical Journal Letters.

Ever since the dawn of the space age, when astronomers glimpsed the first photographs of the far side of the moon, they've wondered why it differed visibly from the near side, particularly in its absence of the dark flat plains called maria, from the Latin for seas. In the new paper, the researchers applied insights from the study of exoplanets that circle close to their stars and, like the moon, are tidally locked, with one half facing ever sunward.

In the immediate aftermath of the giant impact, Ms. Roy said, the Earth would have been as hot as a small sun, which means the half of the moon that faced us would have remained hot as well, while the opposite side had a chance to cool down. Some metals and silicates from the dust cloud surrounding the young orb would preferentially settle onto the cool side, thickening that portion of the crust.

As a result, future meteor impacts on the far side would fail to puncture below the crust, while those hitting the thin-crusted near side would expose the moon's soft inner layers. "The craters would fill with the gooey stuff underneath," Ms. Roy said.

That goo then hardened into maria, the seas we see when we have the good sense to look up and lock eyes with the moon.

Philae Lander Nears a Cosmic Touchdown

BY KENNETH CHANG | NOV. 10, 2014

IN ITS 10-YEAR CHASE of a comet, the European Space Agency's ambitious Rosetta mission has pushed the edges of engineering ingenuity.

After three slingshot flybys of Earth to fling it at ever faster speeds to catch up with its target, Rosetta was so far from the sun that its solar arrays could not generate enough electricity, and it was, by design, put into hibernation for two and a half years.

To the relief of mission managers, Rosetta woke up from its cold, deep sleep as scheduled in January. In August, it finally pulled up alongside the comet, known as 67P/Churyumov-Gerasimenko, both flying closer to the sun at 34,400 miles per hour. In the months since, Rosetta has snapped photographs just 4.5 miles above the craggy surface.

Now it is about to attempt its greatest feat yet: drop a small lander onto the comet.

On Wednesday, at 3:35 a.m. Eastern time, the 220-pound lander, named Philae, is scheduled to detach from Rosetta and be pulled downward by the comet's gravity. Signals from Rosetta will take nearly 30 minutes to travel more than 300 million miles to mission control in Darmstadt, Germany.

Philae will be aimed at a landing site that covers about a third of a square mile; the area looks relatively smooth and clear of boulders but is still close to streams of dust and gas shooting off the surface.

Seven hours later, give or take some minutes, Philae is to bump onto the surface. The comet, 2.5 miles wide, is so small and its gravity so slight that even after that long fall, Philae will be traveling no faster than walking pace.

To keep the lander from bouncing, thrusters will fire for 15 seconds, pressing it against the surface, and a harpoon will shoot into the comet to anchor Philae.

Both the European Space Agency and NASA, which contributed three instruments to the $275 million lander mission, will broadcast coverage on their websites.

In this era of social media and anthropomorphized spacecraft, Philae and Rosetta have their own Twitter feeds: @Philae2014 and @ESA_Rosetta. "I'm so ready!" a Twitter post announced Sunday.

Scientists hope that Philae and its 10 instruments will conduct 64 hours of work before its batteries drain.

After that, if the dust and gas rising from the comet do not obscure too much sunlight, Philae's solar panels are to recharge the batteries enough to provide an hour's worth of observation every couple of days. Engineers expect Philae to survive until next March, when the surface of the comet becomes too hot.

Philae is a high-risk, high-reward gamble. The lander could miss its mark, touch down on a boulder and topple over, or land in shadows where solar arrays cannot produce enough power.

If it succeeds, scientists will have a breathtaking view from the surface of a comet. If it fails, mission managers say, Rosetta will still be a resounding success with the slew of data coming back from the orbiter. Planetary scientists have never had a look at a comet so close up for so long.

Previous spacecraft missions have zoomed by comets at high speeds, providing only brief examinations. By contrast, Rosetta will be a constant companion as Comet 67P approaches the sun, swings around and heads out again, its instruments potentially providing more than two years of data.

"We will watch this comet evolve," Matt Taylor, the project scientist, said during a news briefing last week. "It's never been done before."

Even at its brightest, Comet 67P will not be visible to the naked eye from Earth. At its closest point to the sun, it is still as far away as Earth. At the other end of its 6.5-year orbit, it is as far from the sun as Jupiter.

Still, the changes on Comet 67P have been considerable already. Rosetta initially measured about 0.3 liters of water coming off the comet every second, Dr. Taylor said. "This is increasing," he said. "We're talking of kilos per second now coming off." (A liter of water has a mass of one kilogram.)

By the middle of next year, the comet will be spraying hundreds of liters of water a second, Dr. Taylor said.

The comet has already provided a number of surprising findings, beginning with its shape. Instead of something roughly round, "we saw the duck," Dr. Taylor said, referring to Comet 67P's two-lobed structure that somewhat resembles a rubber bathtub toy.

Among the gases that Rosetta has detected coming off the comet are hydrogen sulfide (the scent of rotten eggs), ammonia, methane, hydrogen cyanide, sulfur dioxide and formaldehyde. "It may be not be the perfume that some of us would choose to wear," Dr. Taylor said. "It's a bit smelly."

He added, "At least there's some alcohol, which some of us might enjoy."

Or not — the alcohol in the comet is methanol, also known as wood alcohol, which is poisonous and can cause blindness when imbibed.

In preparation for the landing operation, Rosetta has moved farther from the comet. On Tuesday, it will take a sharp turn toward the comet on a not-quite collision course.

To get the lander to the selected site, Rosetta will have to drop Philae at the right time at the right spot at an altitude of 14 miles from the comet's center while traveling at the right velocity.

Up to that point, if anything looks not quite right, mission managers have several opportunities to stop and regroup and plan for another day.

But after Philae is let go, the mission managers can only be helpless onlookers. The thrusters are not capable of making any midcourse corrections.

"We cannot actively steer the trajectory of the landing on descent," said Andrea Accomazzo, the flight director. "That's the part that worries me most, because I have no control."

Suddenly, It Seems, Water Is Everywhere in Solar System

BY KENNETH CHANG | MARCH 12, 2015

OCEANS TRAPPED UNDER ICE appear to be pretty common in the solar system and one of them, on a small moon of Saturn's, appears to be quite hot.

This week in the journal Nature, an international team of scientists reported evidence for hydrothermal vents on the Saturnian moon Enceladus, with temperatures of its rocky core surpassing 194 degrees Fahrenheit (90 degrees Celsius) in spots. The discovery, if confirmed, would make Enceladus the only place other than Earth where such chemical reactions between rock and heated water are known to be occurring today — and for many scientists, it would make Enceladus a most promising place to look for life.

"The most surprising part is the high temperature," said Hsiang-Wen Hsu, a scientist at the University of Colorado's Laboratory for Atmospheric and Space Physics and lead author of the paper. "But that's the number we could derive."

Meanwhile, in a paper published Thursday in The Journal of Geophysical Research: Space Physics, another team reported signs of another under-ice ocean, on Ganymede, the largest of Jupiter's moons. Scientists are already convinced that there is a large ocean, also covered by ice, on another Jovian moon, Europa. NASA's Galileo spacecraft had also found hints of hidden water on Ganymede and on another of Jupiter's moons, Callisto.

The new research, using the Hubble Space Telescope, fits with the earlier hints. "This is now stronger evidence for an ocean," said Joachim Saur, a professor of geophysics at the University of Cologne in Germany and the lead author of the Ganymede paper.

"Surprising is the understatement," Christopher P. McKay, a planetary scientist at the NASA Ames Research Center in Mountain View, Calif., said of the multitude of watery moons.

"After spending so many years going after Mars, which is so dry and so bereft of organics and so just plain dead, it's wonderful to go to the outer solar system and find water, water everywhere," said Dr. McKay, who studies the possibility of life on alien worlds. He was not involved in either of the papers.

For the Enceladus findings, Dr. Hsu and his colleagues based their conclusions on minuscule dust particles that NASA's Cassini space-craft encountered as it approached Saturn and after it entered orbit. Instruments on Cassini determined that the particles, less than a millionth of an inch in diameter, were high in silicon but had little or no metals like sodium or magnesium. Dr. Hsu said the dust was probably silica, a molecule of one silicon and two oxygen atoms, the building block of the mineral quartz.

The researchers were also able to trace the dust to Saturn's E Ring, and the material in the E Ring originates from Enceladus, from plumes that emanate near the moon's south pole. "That's the circumstantial part of the work," Dr. Hsu acknowledged.

They performed laboratory experiments to see which conditions could produce the silica particles. The result was alkaline water, with a pH of 8.5 to 10.5, heated to at least 194 degrees. The results fit in with findings last year by other scientists who suggested that Enceladus concealed not just pockets of water but a sea at least as large as Lake Superior.

The mystery is how the interior of Enceladus, just 313 miles wide, grows that hot. A moon that small probably does not have enough radioactive elements at its core to provide continued warmth. A chemical reaction between water and rock called serpentinization could also provide some heat, but the primary mechanism is probably the tidal forces that Saturn exerts on Enceladus.

"The amount of energy being dissipated currently, as well as the location of heating, is not well understood," said Terry A. Hurford, a scientist at NASA's Goddard Space Flight Center in Maryland. "So it is possible that heating can bring water to those temperatures locally."

The earlier evidence for an ocean on Ganymede came from magnetic measurements during flybys by the Galileo probe, which suggested a conductive layer below the surface. Ice is not a good conductor. Saltwater is. But the readings could also be explained by oddities in Ganymede's magnetic field.

In the new research, the Hubble telescope scrutinized Ganymede for seven hours. It could not see below the surface, but it observed the shimmering lights of Ganymede's auroras. As Jupiter rotates, once every 10 hours, its changing magnetic field causes the auroras to sway. If Ganymede were frozen, computer simulations showed, its aurora would sway by 6 degrees. But the salts of an under-ice ocean would generate a counteracting magnetic field, and the auroras would sway by only 2 degrees.

The auroras swayed 2 degrees. "It was exactly like all our computer modeling and all our theory predicted," Dr. Saur said. "It was right on."

The scientists are now applying the approach to Io, a fiery world that certainly does not have an ocean of water. But it might have an underground ocean of magma that would similarly dampen the swaying of auroras. The technique could one day be used to explore planets around distant stars and see if they, too, might have oceans.

As a place for life, Ganymede is less promising, because the ocean looks to be sandwiched between layers of ice and not in contact with rock. By contrast, Enceladus appears to possess all of the necessary ingredients — heat, liquid water and organic molecules — and a future probe could analyze the water by simply flying through the plumes.

"My mantra now is follow the plume," Dr. McKay said.

NASA's Next Horizon in Space

BY MICHAEL ROSTON | AUG. 28, 2015

MOST OF US have come down from the highs of seeing Pluto up close for the first time. Ever since New Horizons beamed back those photos, the question has loomed: What's next?

We asked a few experts and Times readers what NASA's exploratory priority should be in the years ahead. More than 1,600 readers shared their imaginative ideas. Some responses were serious and technical. Others were more whimsical, like that of Carter Read of Brooklyn, who proposed that we "send a record player bumping the sounds of Chuck Berry's 'golden decade' into deep space," because "he's the best communicator the human race has." (Mr. Berry already has one song in space, aboard the Voyager spacecraft.)

Below are some of the best responses, starting with the most popular. Perhaps NASA — and the members of Congress who appropriate its budget — will listen up.

EUROPA, JUPITER'S MOON
The right ingredients for life?

The astrophysicist Neil deGrasse Tyson has been vocal about his choice for future space travel.

"I want to go ice fishing on these icy moons of Jupiter, especially Europa," he said, soon after the Pluto flyby. Nearly one-third of all the responses indicated a readiness for a mission to Europa.

Dr. Tyson and other scientists have long flirted with the idea that Jupiter's moons could harbor the ingredients necessary for life, and this seemed to be the strongest factor motivating readers for a trip to Europa. J. Gradie of Kailua, Hawaii, wrote:

> Europa has the right combination: (a) lots and lots of water, (b) a
> cosmochemical abundance of other essential elements in its large rocky
> core, (c) a liquid water ocean (covered by an icy crust) and (d) a

constant source of energy (tidal heating) operating over billions of years. All this implies a "sea floor" environment analogous to, if not identical to, Earth's mid-ocean ridges. And, we know what's going on down there!

Similar sentiments were offered by other readers:

All our chips should be pooled to answer the question of whether there is life beyond Earth, and Europa is the best place to look. — Peter Dermody, Center Moriches, N.Y.

Readers were also energized by the prospect of doing more than orbiting Europa, with Vivek Vankayalapati of India giving voice to the hope of a submersible vehicle plumbing the moon's watery depths. Such a mission "would spark wonder and awe as well as immense scientific data," he said.

These readers are in luck, sort of. NASA is working on a mission to Europa and already budgeting tens of millions of dollars to plan multiple flybys of the moon with a scientific instrument-packed spacecraft.

The agency may not be able to send a submarine beneath Europa's ice in that mission, planned for the 2020s, but it's a start.

SATURN'S MOONS
"The possibility of life based on a completely different chemical cycle."

Enceladus and Titan, the two moons of Saturn, combined had the second-strongest constituency among Times readers for NASA's next priority. The Cassini mission to Saturn is beginning its goodbye tour after more than a decade of surveying the ringed planet and its moons. Hundreds of readers were motivated to focus in on these two satellites as potential homes for life in the solar system.

Many readers compared Europa and Enceladus and saw the latter as a more likely candidate for life. J. Kent Wallace of NASA's Jet Propulsion Laboratory, speaking on his own behalf, explained why he favored the moon of Saturn over the Jovian body:

1) the ice cap is likely much thinner than on Europa and 2) the radiation environment is much more benign than Europa. Traveling to Saturn takes more time than traveling to Jupiter so it's not an easy choice. However, new technologies would allow us to directly detect microbial life.

And Jack McKever of Flagstaff, Ariz., said that a mission to Enceladus would offer other benefits:

Putting an orbiter around Enceladus would help us to study the composition of its geysers and therefore oceans, but also collect samples of Saturn's E-Ring, which encompasses Enceladus's orbit and consists of ejected material from its geysers. The E-Ring seems basically like a floating library of hundreds of millions of years' worth of frozen samples, which could tell us if life has ever existed on Enceladus.

Saturn's largest moon, Titan, was also of great interest to many readers. Paul Fletcher of Kingston, Wash., offered a thorough case for exploring this moon in favor of others:

Just imagine it — flowing rivers and lakes of methane. Clouds dropping methane rain from the sky. Volcanoes spewing molten water which immediately hardens like lava on the ground. And in the sky there would be Saturn and its rings dominating. It would be on the one hand so familiar and on the other so totally alien it would fire the imagination. Now a lot of people would say Europa because there's a better chance for life, but unless we can send the technology to drill through several miles of solid ice (unlikely), we're not going to find much — maybe sniffing for organic molecules in the plumes of geysers. Now on Titan you have the possibility of life based on a completely different chemical cycle and it would be right on the surface.

A MORE AMBITIOUS MISSION TO MARS

"We'd better explore whether we can create a backup."

One out of every 10 readers who responded was intent on greater exploration of Mars than NASA has already completed. A common theme among these readers was the fragility of life on Earth. With Mars, they argued, we might learn more about what fate our planet could face if it was not cared for, or create a backup in case our world was to become too far gone to save.

The case for deeper exploration of Mars to help our own planet was summarized by Jeff Ferrell of Portland, Ore.:

Visiting Mars could be like visiting the Earth a billion years from now. A closer inspection could reveal that Mars (a billion years ago) was once an Earth-like planet, replete with an atmosphere, greenhouse effect, liquid water, and possibly even life. It could also offer relevant insight to Earth sciences, and even clues as to the inevitable geologic death of our own home planet.

And the worry that we needed another home for humanity was concisely summarized by Lincoln Konkle of New Jersey, who wrote, "Let's face it: we're wrecking the Earth's climate and environment, and not making much progress to change our ways, so we'd better explore whether we can create a backup."

While there are quite a few challenges to putting people on Mars, Max Blum of Dallas offered this upbeat assessment of the prospects, and tried to put its distance from our world in perspective:

It is not as close as the Moon, obviously, but close enough for our rudimentary space vehicle science: 180 days traveling at a nominal 50,000 km/hr. In a historical context, that is less than the time it took Europeans to sail to Asia in the 1500's.

Mars already has a prominent place in NASA's plans in the decades ahead. Beyond the current Curiosity rover's exploration of the planet, the Mars 2020 mission is a more concrete effort to land additional technology on the red planet. Others like the plan for the Orion spacecraft to study an asteroid that will be made to orbit our moon are being pursued in part to prepare for future manned missions to Mars. NASA and other space agencies also published a road map in 2013 that includes more extensive plans for exploring our sun's fourth satellite.

OUR OFT OVERLOOKED NEIGHBOR VENUS
Technological and musical arguments for exploration.

Our solar system's second planet does not receive a great deal of attention. A sense of cosmic injustice drove some of the interest in Venus, highlighted by one of the respondents who said it warranted greater exploration. "It is really unfair to go for exploration of new horizons while we know less about our closest neighbor," wrote Sayyed Mohammad Abtahi of Uppsala, Sweden.

David Pieri of NASA's Jet Propulsion Laboratory, speaking on his own behalf, focused on the feasibility of a visit:

Technology is even now being developed to allow us to persist on the hellish Venusian surface and float or fly through its atmosphere, so we should go.

Al Davis of Hyannis, Neb., proposed seeding the planet with life that could thrive in its atmosphere, while John Ferrara called for sending a vessel into its atmosphere to study its climate "as a persistent weather station":

Temperatures at 50km above the ground are a pleasant 60-80 degrees fahrenheit, and the air pressure is similar to Earth's at sea level. An airship could inflate as it parachutes though the relatively thick upper atmosphere, slowing the craft long enough for it to buoy its own weight before dipping dangerously low.

And one reader offered a musical reason for exploring Venus. "If Frankie Avalon (1959), Shocking Blue (1970) and Bananarama (1986) all can croon to it over the airwaves," Jim Swenson of Dubuque, Iowa, wrote, "surely we can visit Venus to see if there's more to it than meets the eye."

THE MOON
"Why not focus on what's right next door?"

Remember the moon? You may see it every night and not take much interest in it, but a wide variety of Times readers wanted more from our planet's largest satellite. Many of their hopes for lunar exploration were reminiscent of what NASA officials dreamed would happen in the decade after Neil and Buzz first set foot on that rock. In some cases, the reasoning for focusing on the moon was purely practical, like that of Ken from New Jersey:

> We're getting ahead of ourselves. If we are trying to lay a foundation for space travel/exploration years and years from now, why not focus on what's right next door? If we can figure out how to get to and from the Moon routinely and establish a lunar base there "cheaply," then Mars and all the others won't be far behind.

Jordan Turner of Kansas City, Mo., made a plea that was every bit as passionate, if not quite as practical.

"Please do this in my lifetime. I'm 32," he wrote. "I would love to say I've been to the moon and stayed at the Hilton Moon Inn and had moons over my hammy at the Denny's there before I went outside for a moon walk."

THE LONG-TERM PLANNERS' OPTION: EXOPLANETS
"We have to start sometime."

For a passionate subset of Times readers, ideas started to fly at warp speeds when their imaginations were loosed beyond the boundaries of our solar system. Many were energized at the prospect of constructing a "starshade" to help telescopes study exoplanets in other star systems. And plenty offered ambitious ideas for a distant time in the future when humanity can visit one of those planets.

Keith Spencer of Oakland, Calif., was content with an unmanned mission to our star's nearest neighbor, Alpha Centauri:

> Though it would take thousands of years to reach, the engineering challenges, and the generations it would inspire, would prove that humans are capable of thinking long-term, beyond the next congressional budget, beyond our own lifespans, even beyond our civilizations. Such a mission would return unprecedented science and transcend petty nationalisms, since it is unknown if the United States would still exist that far in the future. For both social and scientific reasons, an interstellar mission to Alpha Centauri would be the next giant leap for mankind.

William LeGro of Silver Lake, Calif., emphasized the importance of simply getting started.

We need to spend serious effort, resources and money on developing a propulsion system that would get us there — the Alcubierre warp drive, light sails, antimatter engines. No, of course none of those are possible — NOW. But in 1930 reaching Pluto wasn't possible either. In fact, these drive systems all have a greater or lesser degree of possibility. We won't know how much until we begin to devise them — and that process will likely lead us to other possibilities, maybe a different but more promising star. Reaching the nearest star is less a matter of ability and more a matter of will. We just have to decide we're going to do it, and we will succeed. We have to start sometime.

THE ICY GIANTS
Sharing our affections with Uranus and Neptune.

Jupiter and Saturn, the gas giants, are something like our solar systems' favored children. Their ice giant siblings, Uranus and Neptune, have received much less attention over the course of our explorations of the planets. A significant group of readers wanted to rectify that.

Of the two planets, interest in Uranus was greater. Marjorie Parent-Greenman of Ann Arbor, Mich., explained what fired her imagination with a number of questions: "It's the only planet, in our solar system, with a tilted axis. How, or why, did that happen? Has it always been tilted? If not, what caused it?" Lucas, a 7-year-old also in Ann Arbor, wrote, "It's so colorful and beautiful, and it's interesting to learn about a colorful and beautiful planet."

Another reader, Dan Moss in Dallas, offered a more novel justification for studying the seventh planet from the sun:

That unfortunate name — Uranus — has made a perfectly fine planet the butt of every schoolyard joke and late-nite wisecrack in English. Nothing would rehabilitate poor Uranus like a proper, awesome visit.

BEYOND PLUTO
There are more (dwarf) planets left to explore.

The solar system doesn't end at Pluto. The objects that lie in the Kuiper Belt — the icy objects beyond the orbit of Neptune — and the Oort Cloud — an even more distant agglomeration of icy bodies — fascinated a vocal group of readers. "Simply put: it is the least known part of our solar system," wrote Ashraf Mourad of New York. William J. Swiggard of Hatfield, Mass. added: "The Pluto System is only a tiny fraction of what's out there in a tantalizing, vast, dark system exceedingly difficult to study from earth. These bodies are the 'leftovers of creation' dating from the time our solar system formed."

Francis Wilkin of Schenectady, N.Y., called for a mission to Eris, the dwarf planet in the Kuiper Belt that helped downgrade Pluto from planet to dwarf. "A mission to Eris combats the idea that we've already visited all the (traditional 9) planets, with no major worlds left to explore," he wrote. "Being more massive than Pluto, this is a significant world with mysteries to uncover, especially how it formed so far out."

It is possible that New Horizons, the spacecraft that sent back all of the amazing imagery from Pluto and its moons, could study some Kuiper Belt objects with its remaining power. Whether NASA will make resources available for that mission remains an open question.

ASTEROIDS
"We have never visited a metal body."

A vocal group of readers expressed eagerness for the exploration of objects in the asteroid belt between Mars and Jupiter. While NASA's Dawn mission continues to explore the dwarf planet Ceres in the asteroid belt, they offered additional ideas.

Paul Lozancich of Fair Oaks, Calif., wrote that asteroids "could be communications posts, mining colonies and way stations. Small ones could be hollowed out, outfitted with sails or huge rockets and used as a giant bus to shuttle between planets in the solar system."

Others were impressed by the uniqueness of objects in the asteroid belt, like the body known as Psyche. Lindy Elkins-Tanton, a planetary scientist at Arizona State University, explained why Psyche charged up her imagination:

The only place in the solar system where humankind can visit a metal planetary core! We've visited rocky, gassy and icy bodies. We have never visited a metal body. What will it look like? Psyche will teach us about the earliest parts of planetary accretion, and how terrestrial planets become what they are.

ASHAKI LLOYD provided additional research.

Cassini Seeks Insights to Life in Plumes of Enceladus, Saturn's Icy Moon

BY DENNIS OVERBYE | OCT. 28, 2015

WHERE THERE IS WATER, is there life?

That's the $64 billion question now facing NASA and the rest of lonely humanity. When the New Horizons spacecraft, cameras clicking, sped past Pluto in July, it represented an inflection point in the conquest of the solar system. Half a century after the first planetary probe sailed past Venus, all the planets and would-be planets we have known and loved, and all the marvelous rocks and snowballs circling them, have been detected and inspected, reconnoitered.

That part of human history, the astrophysical exploration of the solar system, is over. The next part, the biological exploration of space, is just beginning. We have finished counting the rocks in the neighborhood. It is time to find out if anything is living on them, a job that could easily take another half century.

NASA's mantra for finding alien life has long been to "follow the water," the one ingredient essential to our own biochemistry. On Wednesday, NASA sampled the most available water out there, as the Cassini spacecraft plunged through an icy spray erupting from the little Saturnian moon Enceladus.

Enceladus is only 300 miles across and whiter than a Bing Crosby Christmas, reflecting virtually all the sunlight that hits it, which should make it colder and deader than Scrooge's heart.

But in 2005, shortly after starting an 11-year sojourn at Saturn, Cassini recorded jets of water squirting from cracks known as tiger stripes near the south pole of Enceladus — evidence, scientists say, of an underground ocean kept warm and liquid by tidal flexing of the little moon as it is stretched and squeezed by Saturn.

And with that, Enceladus leapfrogged to the top of astrobiologists' list of promising places to look for life. If there is life in its ocean, alien microbes could be riding those geysers out into space where a passing spacecraft could grab them. No need to drill through miles of ice or dig up rocks.

As Chris McKay, an astrobiologist at NASA's Ames Research Center, said, it's as if nature had hung up a sign at Enceladus saying "Free Samples."

Discovering life was not on the agenda when Cassini was designed and launched two decades ago. Its instruments can't capture microbes or detect life, but in a couple of dozen passes through the plumes of Enceladus, it has detected various molecules associated with life: water vapor, carbon dioxide, methane, molecular nitrogen, propane, acetylene, formaldehyde and traces of ammonia.

Wednesday's dive was the deepest Cassini will make through the plumes, only 30 miles above the icy surface. Scientists are especially interested in measuring the amount of hydrogen gas in the plume, which would tell them how much energy and heat are being generated by chemical reactions in hydrothermal vents at the bottom of the moon's ocean.

It is in such ocean vents that some of the most primordial-looking life-forms have been found on our own planet. What the Cassini scientists find out could help set the stage for a return mission with a spacecraft designed to detect or even bring back samples of life.

These are optimistic, almost sci-fi times. The fact that life was present on Earth as early as 4.1 billion years ago — pretty much as soon as asteroids and leftover planet junk stopped bombarding the new Earth and let it cool down — has led astrobiologists to conclude that, given the right conditions, life will take hold quickly. Not just in our solar system, but in some of the thousands of planetary systems that Kepler and other missions squinting at distant stars have uncovered.

And if water is indeed the key, the solar system has had several chances to get lucky. Besides Enceladus, there is an ocean underneath the ice of Jupiter's moon Europa, and the Hubble Space Telescope has hinted that it too is venting into space. NASA has begun planning for a mission next decade to fly by it.

And of course there's Mars, with its dead oceans and intriguing streaks of damp sand, springboard of a thousand sci-fi invasions of Earth, but in recent decades the target of robot invasions going the other direction.

Some scientists even make the case that genesis happened not on Earth but on Mars. Our biochemical ancestors would then have made the passage on an asteroid, making us all Martians and perhaps explaining our curious attraction to the Red Planet.

And then there is Titan, Saturn's largest moon, the only moon in the solar system with a thick atmosphere and lakes on its surface, except that in this case the liquid in them is methane and the beaches and valleys are made of hydrocarbon slush.

NASA's working definition of life, coined by a group of biologists in 1992, is "a self-sustaining chemical system capable of Darwinian evolution."

Any liquid could serve as the medium of this thing, process, whatever it is. Life on Titan would expand our notions of what is biochemically possible out there in the rest of the universe.

Our history of exploration suggests that surprise is the nature of the game. That was the lesson of the Voyager missions: Every world or moon encountered on that twin-spacecraft odyssey was different, an example of the laws of physics sculpted by time and circumstance into unique and weird forms.

And so far that is the lesson of the new astronomy of exoplanets — thousands of planetary systems, but not a single one that looks like our own.

The detection of a single piece of pond slime, one alien microbe, on some other world would rank as one of the greatest discoveries in the history of science. Why should we expect it to look anything like what we already know?

That microbe won't come any cheaper than the Higgs boson, the keystone of modern particle physics, which cost more than $10 billion to hunt down over half a century.

Finding that microbe will involve launching big, complicated chunks of hardware to various corners of the solar system, and that means work for engineers, scientists, accountants, welders, machinists, electricians, programmers and practitioners of other crafts yet to be invented — astro-robot-paleontologists, say.

However many billions of dollars it takes to knock on doors and find out if anybody is at home, it will all be spent here on Earth, on people and things we all say we want: innovation, education, science, technology.

We've seen this have a happy ending before. It was the kids of the aerospace industry and the military-industrial complex, especially in California, who gave us Silicon Valley and general relativity in our pockets.

In this era, a happy ending could include the news that we are not alone, that the cosmos is more diverse, again, than we had imagined.

Or not.

In another 50 years the silence from out there could be deafening.

Venus: Inhospitable, and Perhaps Instructional

BY KENNETH CHANG | OCT. 17, 2016

VENUS IS NOT a placid paradise — that much we know. In addition to searing surface temperatures, wind in the upper atmosphere howls at up to 250 miles per hour, carrying clouds around the planet once every four days.

Yet Venus itself spins very slowly: one rotation every 243 Earth days — in the wrong direction, no less, opposite to almost every other body in the solar system.

On the whole, the atmosphere on Earth rotates about the same speed as the planet. So why does the air on slow-spinning Venus speed around so much faster than the planet itself?

The Japanese space probe Akatsuki, now in orbit around Venus, seeks to solve the mystery of so-called super-rotation. Scientists working on the mission are presenting some of their early findings at a meeting this week of the American Astronomical Society's Division for Planetary Sciences in Pasadena, Calif.

That is not just an idle trivia question for planetary scientists. Computer models of our own weather fail when applied to Venus, and knowledge of the planet's workings could better our understanding of Earth's.

"We don't know what is the missing point in meteorology," said Masato Nakamura, Akatsuki's project manager. "If we know what makes such a super-rotation, we will have a much deeper understanding of the atmospheric dynamics, not just on Venus but also on Earth. We will learn much more about the Earth climate."

In recent years, Venus has been a backwater of planetary exploration, even though it is much closer in size to Earth than is Mars. For a long time, scientists imagined there could be a habitable tropical paradise beneath Venus's thick clouds.

In the late 1950s, intense thermal emissions, measured by a radio telescope on Earth, told a different story. Venus broils.

The average surface temperature is more than 850 degrees Fahrenheit — an extreme demonstration of the heat-trapping prowess of carbon dioxide, the primary constituent of the Venusian atmosphere. Clouds of sulfuric acid make it an even less appealing place to visit.

In the 1990s, NASA's Magellan spacecraft precisely mapped the topography of Venus through radar. Except for a few flybys by spacecraft on the way to somewhere else, NASA has not returned to Venus, although the agency is considering two modest proposals.

A European mission, Venus Express, studied the planet from 2006 to 2014, discovering among other things a frigid layer of atmosphere, minus 280 degrees Fahrenheit at an altitude of 75 miles, sandwiched between two warmer layers.

But now Akatsuki, which entered orbit last December, has begun its work. Takehiko Satoh, one of the mission scientists, said that one of "the most exciting, most surprising results" so far came almost immediately after the spacecraft arrived.

The camera that captures long-wavelength infrared light from the cloud tops discovered an arc-shaped white streak that stretched some 6,000 miles from nearly the south pole to nearly the north pole.

Curiously, this giant atmospheric feature does not move with the atmosphere. "It seems to be fixed to the ground," Dr. Satoh said.

The arc sits above Aphrodite Terra, a highland region about the size of Africa that rises up to three miles from the surface. Scientists working on data from the Venus Express reported a similar finding in July.

One possibility is that as the wind blows over Aphrodite Terra, clouds are pushed higher and the temperature of the cloud tops falls. "Our interpretation is there is some disturbance from the high mountain," Dr. Nakamura said.

Dr. Satoh said there were primarily two competing ideas for where the energy for the Venus wind comes from. One is that energy coming from the sun accelerates the wind. The second is that atmosphere is so thick that it gradually slows down the spinning of the planet, and that angular momentum is transferred to the air.

According to this theory, even though breezes on the surface are slight — a couple of miles per hour — the speeds increase at higher altitudes as the air thins.

The small spacecraft — the main body is a box a bit bigger than a refrigerator — carries five cameras, collecting light at different wavelengths to monitor the Venusian atmosphere at different altitudes.

In another experiment, scientists will observe how the radio signal from the spacecraft to Earth is distorted when it passes through the atmosphere. That will reveal temperature, abundance of sulfuric acid vapor and other properties. By observing the atmosphere at different altitudes, they can detect wavelike features that rise and fall, like blobs in a lava lamp.

"If the solar heating or thermal tide hypothesis is correct," Dr. Satoh said, "we may see different propagation of the wave, from cloud top to the lower level." If the viscosity theory is correct, the waves should propagate in the opposite direction, from the ground to the clouds.

Perhaps the answers will become clear in a year — or maybe four. "We need to analyze a lot of big data," Dr. Nakamura said.

That Akatsuki, which means "dawn" in Japanese, is there at all is the result of ingenuity and perseverance.

It launched in May 2010 and arrived at Venus seven months later. But when its main engine failed to fire properly, it sailed right past the planet.

"It was a very sad moment," Dr. Satoh said.

Within a day, Dr. Satoh said, calculations indicated that in six years, Akatsuki, in orbit around the sun instead of Venus, could meet up with Venus again. But it was not clear the spacecraft still would be able to slow down and enter orbit.

An investigation found that a valve in the engine had leaked, leading to the formation of salts that fused it shut. The engine, as it fired, had overheated beyond repair.

Akatsuki still had the maneuvering thrusters that were to be used after it entered orbit. They were not as powerful as the broken engine, but they could apply enough force to slow it down enough so that Venus' gravity could capture it.

Because of worries that the longer stay in space, with the bombardment of solar radiation and cosmic rays, would degrade the instruments, the craft was maneuvered so the second rendezvous would occur a year earlier, in November 2015.

Then calculations suggested that orbit might not be stable, and the spacecraft might crash into Venus shortly afterward. Another adjustment pushed the arrival back a couple of weeks to Dec. 7, exactly five years after the original arrival date.

This time, everything worked.

The Akatsuki's orbit is different from the one originally envisioned. Instead of being synchronized to the spinning atmosphere, which would have allowed scientists to better track small changes, the spacecraft now loops around Venus in a large elliptical orbit.

That provides different benefits. Instead of intently staring at one spot, seeing the smallest changes, scientists are now able to see what happens on a global scale, although they will miss some of the details.

Akatsuki is to continue operating until at least April 2018, depending on how much fuel it has left. "We know at least we have one kilogram of fuel," said Dr. Nakamura, likening the uncertainty to an imprecise fuel gauge in a car.

If it turns out that Akatsuki has more, the spacecraft could continue operating for perhaps up to six years, he said.

An Interstellar Visitor Both Familiar and Alien

BY DENNIS OVERBYE | NOV. 22, 2017

VISIT THE GALAXY before the galaxy visits you.

This fall, the galaxy came calling in the form of a small reddish cigar-shaped object named Oumuamua by astronomers based in Hawaii. They discovered it in October, careening through the solar system at 40,000 miles an hour, an interstellar emissary from points unknown.

Oumuamua (Oh-moo-a-moo-a), Hawaiian for "scout" or "messenger," was not here long.

It was first noticed zooming out of the constellation Lyra on Oct. 19, about 20 million miles from Earth. By next May, it will already be passing Jupiter on its way out of the solar system.

The asteroid brought shades of Arthur C. Clarke's novel "Rendezvous With Rama," in which explorers find and board an empty alien spacecraft sailing through the solar system. Or perhaps even reminders of the monoliths that power human evolution in "2001: A Space Odyssey."

The discovery set off a worldwide scramble for telescope time to observe the object. Astronomers from the SETI Institute even got into the act, swinging into action to look for alien radio signals Just In Case.

For now, however, those are just science fiction thrills. "Our observations are entirely consistent with it being a natural object," said Karen Meech of the University of Hawaii's Institute for Astronomy and leader of the international collaboration that discovered Oumuamua with the Pan-STARRS 1 telescope on Haleakala, Maui.

Dr. Meech's team has now published the first report of their observations in Nature. The paper describes the interstellar visitor as both reassuringly familiar and utterly alien.

"We don't see anything like that in our solar system," Dr. Meech said.

In its color and other imputed properties, Oumuamua resembles the asteroids we already know and fear will one day smash the Earth and human civilization to smithereens.

But the asteroid's shape is weird. It is extremely elongated, at least 10 times as long as it is wide, perhaps 800 yards by 80 yards.

Though the mysterious object is nearly gone, thousands like it probably lurk unsuspected and undetected in our solar system, according to the scientists.

The Pan-STARRS telescope was built to patrol the sky for dangerous asteroids in our own system, not interlopers from beyond. But astronomers got a surprise.

Dr. Meech learned in a phone call one night that her colleagues had found one whose path seemed to originate beyond the solar system altogether. "Wow, this is exciting," Dr. Meech recalled thinking.

Astronomers had long surmised that interstellar debris might invade the solar system from time to time, in the form of icy chunks spit from the rocky disks forming faraway planets.

Such wanderers would manifest themselves as comets when they got close to our sun, vaporizing and lighting up; however, they have not been seen. Now astronomers know why.

Oumuamua showed no such cometary brightening. It is so dark and faint that it could only have been detected by a powerful telescope with a wide field of view, like Pan-STARRS.

Many more should be visible to the Large Synoptic Survey Telescope, with a diameter of eight meters, being built in Chile. "We have to get ready for these," Dr. Meech said.

Oumuamua brightens and dims dramatically every 7.3 hours, which suggests that it is rotating about its short axis. That is something the little asteroid could endure without flying apart only if it were made of sterner, stronger stuff than the dirty snow that characterizes most comets.

Spectral measurements have revealed that Oumuamua is dark red, the color of many moons of the outer solar system on which icy organic molecules have been stained by radiation in outer space. Iron can also contribute that color, Dr. Meech said.

How Oumuamua got its shape is a mystery for now. Perhaps, Dr. Meech said, it was shot away from its home star by a supernova explosion. Or perhaps it was formed by a pair of objects that collided and stuck together. Stay tuned.

Where did it come from? Dr. Meech said the astronomers were initially excited when the orbit appeared to point to the brightest star in Lyra, Vega, which is known to have a debris disk. It would have taken the object about 600,000 years to get here from there, astronomers estimated.

But further refinements in the trajectory have made it less likely that Vega actually was the source.

The fact that Oumuamua was traveling at about the same speed relative to the sun as other nearby stars suggests that this is the asteroid's first encounter with a new star system.

Still, the authors write in Nature, "The possibility that Oumuamua has been orbiting the galaxy for billions of years cannot be ruled out."

Where it's going is equally in the dark. Like the Voyager spacecraft slingshotted around Jupiter, Oumuamua will leave the sun with more energy and heading in a different direction, Dr. Meech said.

The adventures of this asteroid and its ilk paint a very different picture of the galaxy than you might imagine while gazing up at a sky in which the stars seem separate and sovereign, beaming away in solitude.

The oxygen and iron in our blood were created in a supernova explosion long ago and far away from here, and the gold in our wedding bands was formed in the collision of neutron stars. We now know that meteorites sprung by asteroid impacts on Mars land on Earth all the time.

Otherwise respectable astronomers speculate that one of them might have seeded Earth with life that started on Mars when it was warm and wet long ago.

But we can look even further out and backward in time for our connection to the cosmos. Consider the hundreds of thousands of years that Oumuamua might have taken to get here. While that might sound like a long time, it is a blink of cosmic time.

The Milky Way galaxy is 10 billion years old. Which means that over the course of our galaxy's lifetime so far, little Oumuamua might have cruised through some 20,000 star systems — a small fraction of the 200 billion stars in the galaxy, but still a goodly number of stamps on its cosmic passport.

Oumuamua would have trailed behind bits of dust and debris, and so the stars and the worlds of the galaxy mix it up. It may be that the universe is a small place after all.

Asteroids and Adversaries: Challenging What NASA Knows About Space Rocks

BY KENNETH CHANG | JUNE 14, 2018

Two years ago, NASA dismissed and mocked an amateur's criticisms of its asteroids database. Now Nathan Myhrvold is back, and his papers have passed peer review.

THOUSANDS OF ASTEROIDS are passing through Earth's neighborhood all the time. Although the odds of a direct hit on the planet any time soon are slim, even a small asteroid the size of a house could explode with as much energy as an atomic bomb.

So scientists at NASA are charged with scanning the skies for such dangerous space rocks. If one were on a collision course with our planet, information about how big it is and what it's made of would be essential for deflecting it, or calculating the destruction if it hits.

For the last couple of years, Nathan P. Myhrvold, a former chief technologist at Microsoft with a physics doctorate from Princeton, has roiled the small, congenial community of asteroid scientists by saying they know less than they think about these near-Earth objects. He argues that a trove of data from NASA they rely on is flawed and unreliable.

Since 2011, a NASA project known as Neowise has cataloged the sizes and reflectivity of 158,000 asteroids, and it claimed that its diameter estimates were often within 10 percent of the actual size. Dr. Myhrvold said the uncertainties were much greater, largely because NASA researchers were using data from a satellite designed for observing distant objects, not nearby asteroids. "The science is terrible," he said.

Now his arguments have been published in Icarus, one of planetary science's most prestigious journals.

"I've gotten people to agree I was right," Dr. Myhrvold said.

Dr. Myhrvold, with a personal collection of meteorites, has followed an eclectic career since leaving Microsoft.

When Dr. Myhrvold first revealed his research in 2016, NASA said that it had not been through scientific peer review. Two years later, the agency is still defending the results of the mission.

"The Neowise team stands by its data and scientific findings that have been published in several peer-reviewed journal articles," the agency said in a statement. "NASA is confident the processes and analyses performed by the Neowise team are valid, as verified by independent researchers."

In an email, Edward L. Wright, a University of California, Los Angeles scientist who served as the principal investigator for the Wide-field Infrared Survey Explorer, or WISE, the mission that Neowise grew out of, disputed some technical aspects of Dr. Myhrvold's paper. He said one section about the error analysis was "a waste of paper."

He did not respond to further emails.

Dr. Myhrvold's findings pose a challenge to a proposed NASA asteroid-finding mission called Neocam, short for Near-Earth Object Camera, which would likely cost hundreds of millions of dollars. A congressional committee that controls NASA's purse strings just included $10 million more in a budget bill for the development of Neocam.

The same scientist, Amy Mainzer of NASA's Jet Propulsion Laboratory in Pasadena, Calif., is the principal investigator for both Neowise and Neocam. NASA said she was unavailable for comment.

At least one scientist at NASA found merit in Dr. Myhrvold's pursuit. David Morrison, a planetary scientist at the space agency's Ames Research Center in Mountain View, Calif., said of the scientific issues raised in the papers: "For the most part, I think Myhrvold is correct."

"I do think it's valuable for someone, a smart outsider, to go in and analyze data that are important," said Dr. Morrison, who is not involved with Dr. Myhrvold's research or Neowise. "That has to help science. That cannot be a bad thing."

'DUMB THINGS' IN THE DATA

The squabble revolves around data collected by NASA's WISE spacecraft, which scanned the skies beginning in 2009, taking pictures of hundreds of millions of distant galaxies and stars.

Asteroids were also whizzing through WISE's field of view, and the Neowise project was established to analyze them.

By looking at heat radiated by asteroids, it is possible to estimate an asteroid's size and the reflectivity of its surface. The Neowise data is by far the largest collection, and hundreds of scientific papers have cited those findings.

When Dr. Myhrvold made his initial claims, the Neowise scientists made fun of a few errors like an equation that mixed up radius and diameter.

"It is too bad Myhrvold doesn't have Google's bug-finding bounty policy," Dr. Wright told Scientific American. "If he did, I'd be rich."

Dr. Mainzer also said at the time, "We believe at this point it's best to allow the process of peer review — the foundation of the scientific process — to move forward."

Dr. Myhrvold has followed an eclectic career since leaving Microsoft nearly two decades ago. He has gained renown for a six-volume cookbook called "Modernist Cuisine," and he has been scorned for the work of his company, Intellectual Ventures, which buys patents and collects licensing fees. He is also an avid digger of dinosaur fossils, with a number of published paleontology papers.

Earlier this year, Icarus published Dr. Myhrvold's first paper on how reflected sunlight affects measurements of asteroids at the shorter infrared wavelengths measured by WISE. It has now accepted and posted a second paper last month containing Dr. Myhrvold's criticisms of the NASA asteroid data.

Among them is the case of the copied numbers.

The Neowise researchers' model was calibrated with diameters for about a hundred asteroids that have been measured by radar, visiting spacecraft or when an asteroid passed in front of a distant star.

When the scientists reported their findings, they did not include the estimates produced by their models, which would have given a sense of how good the model is. Instead they included the earlier measurements.

Other astronomers agreed that the Neowise scientists were not clear about what numbers they were reporting.

"They did some kind of dumb things," said Alan W. Harris, a retired NASA asteroid expert who was one of the reviewers of Dr. Myhrvold's second paper.

Dr. Myhrvold has accused the Neowise scientists of going into a NASA archive of planetary results, changing some of the copied numbers and deleting others without giving notice.

"They went back and rewrote history," he said. "What it shows is even this far in, they're still lying. They haven't come clean."

Dr. Harris said he did not see nefarious behavior by the Neowise scientists, but agreed, "That's still weird."

Dr. Myhrvold also contends that Neowise set up arbitrary rules for deciding which data to keep and disregard and that they did not describe their methods in enough detail for other scientists to replicate.

RANCOR AND REPLICATION

The tussle has spilled from scientific journals and conferences into contentious letters from lawyers. Dr. Myhrvold has filed Freedom of Information Act requests for information and algorithms that he said would be needed to properly check the Neowise findings.

Dr. Myhrvold said NASA and Congress should put planning for the proposed Neocam spacecraft on hold, because it could suffer from the same shortfalls as Neowise. "Why does it get to avoid further scrutiny and just get money directly from Congress?" he asked.

He also said a ground-based observatory, the Large Synoptic Survey Telescope, already under construction, will accomplish much of Neocam's mission.

In his email, Dr. Wright said Dr. Myhrvold had taken an "adversarial approach." Dr. Myhrvold, in turn, noted Dr. Wright's earlier disparaging comments.

This rancor perplexes other asteroid researchers.

"It's a strange story," Dr. Morrison said. "I've never experienced anything like this in my field."

The editors of Icarus now anticipate a rebuttal by Dr. Mainzer after she initially passed on an invitation several months ago to write one.

In June, NASA put out a news release about a different paper, also accepted by Icarus, by a team of European scientists. They used a more sophisticated method to calculate the sizes of more than 100 asteroids and the results largely matched the Neowise estimates.

But the analysis was limited to asteroids with the most reliable long-wavelength infrared measurements by WISE, a tiny fraction of the 158,000 that Neowise had analyzed.

In follow-up research, Dr. Myhrvold wants to show how the work of Neowise could be better done. He has started collaborating with

Jean-Luc Margot, the chairman of the earth, planetary and space sciences department at U.C.L.A. and a colleague of Dr. Wright's. (Dr. Myhrvold has also given $350,000 to the university, his alma mater. The money will support graduate student research in Dr. Margot's department, although not necessarily on asteroids.)

Dr. Margot said that in preliminary work, he and his students have already reproduced some of Dr. Myhrvold's results.

Unlike Dr. Myhrvold, Dr. Margot said he has had productive conversations with Dr. Wright and others from Neowise. "I have not detected any discomfort," Dr. Margot said. "I start from the assumption that everyone wants the best out of the data."

Dr. Myhrvold thinks there are discoveries in the Neowise data, hidden in what was thrown away during the analysis. "Maybe there are new classes of asteroids out there," he said. "This is the only thing we're going to have for a long time. We ought to get it right."

CHAPTER 5

Life on Mars, Human and Otherwise

Of the subjects for space research, Mars holds some of the deepest and longest-held interest. Our neighboring Red Planet has been an object of careful research and intense speculation as a place for human colonization and a candidate for the origin of Earthly life. As rover missions to Mars have charted the planet's terrain, the discovery of flowing water has raised the possibility of life-forms still present there. Meanwhile, Earth-bound researchers prepare for the day when humans first set foot on Mars.

A Far-Flung Possibility for the Origin of Life

BY CARL ZIMMER | SEPT. 12, 2013

"WE'RE ALL MARTIANS, SCIENTIST CLAIMS," The Telegraph wrote on Aug. 28. Similar articles showed up in newspapers and on Web sites around the world.

The scientist who inspired all the headlines is a chemist named Steven Benner. Headlines notwithstanding, Dr. Benner is not a wild-eyed U.F.O. advocate claiming to have seen Little Green Men. Instead, he is one of the world's leading experts on the origin of life.

"Steve is one of the master organic chemists tackling this problem," said Robert M. Hazen, a mineralogist at the Carnegie Institution and the author of "The Story of Earth."

The cause for Dr. Benner's new-found celebrity is a lecture he delivered at a geology conference in Florence, Italy, on Aug. 29. During his talk, he did not wave satellite pictures of canals on Mars, or of Martian hills that vaguely look like a human face.

Instead, he challenged his fellow scientists to look hard at the evidence we have about how life began.

Depending on how you view that evidence, Dr. Benner argued, Mars might be a more likely place for life to have started than Earth. The best way to determine the actual answer, Dr. Benner argued, is to look for certain types of chemicals on both planets.

"I really don't have a dog in this fight," said Dr. Benner, a distinguished fellow at the Westheimer Institute at the Foundation for Applied Molecular Evolution in Gainesville, Fla., in a telephone interview after he returned from Italy. "It could go either way and I would be equally happy."

Over the past few years, Dr. Benner and his colleagues have amassed evidence for one potential path by which chemicals could have become living matter. Small organic compounds could have reacted with each other to produce string-shaped, self-replicating molecules.

These strands, known as RNA, later combined into double-strands: the DNA in which we and other species encode our genes.

In chemical experiments, Dr. Benner and his colleagues have demonstrated the occurrence of many of the reactions in this path. But they've also discovered roadblocks. For instance, the precursors to RNA can bond in a lot of ways, some good and some bad. While some reactions can lead organic molecules toward RNA, many others can turn them into gooey tar.

Dr. Benner and his colleagues discovered that minerals containing borate could help life overcome this obstacle. Binding to the precursors of RNA, borate blocks them from reacting in destructive ways, so they are much more likely to form compounds that could eventually give rise to life.

But even in the presence of borate, Dr. Benner and his colleagues have found, these precursors can't make some of the final changes that turn them into RNA. And just recently the researchers found a way out of this bind. Molybdate minerals can react with the precursors to help them become RNA.

While this chemistry may work in the lab, however, it may not have worked on the early Earth. Dr. Hazen and other geologists have argued that it's unlikely that borate or molybdate were abundant on the planet.

Today, borate is found in deserts that formed after large seas evaporated. But deserts may not have existed four billion years ago. A number of studies suggest that the early Earth was covered in water and had few if any continents.

As for molybdate, it only forms in the presence of oxygen. The atmosphere of the early Earth appears to have been nearly oxygen-free.

At the moment, Mars looks more promising to Dr. Benner. The evidence gathered by satellites and rovers suggests that both oceans and continents existed early in the planet's lifetime. Under those conditions, borate might have formed.

Just this June, some more evidence emerged that supports this idea. Studying a meteorite from Mars, scientists at the University of Hawaii reported that it contained high levels of boron, a component of borate.

The atmosphere of early Mars also shows signs of having contained oxygen, enabling molybdate to form. With a supply of both borate and molybdate, Mars might have been a favorable place for RNA to emerge, and for life to start. A giant impact on the Red Planet could then have kicked up microbe-laden rocks, which later fell to Earth.

In his recent lecture, Dr. Benner did not present this argument as proof that we are Martians. Instead, he offered a way to organize our thinking about the origin of life. One of his lecture slides was entitled "A Logic Tree." It displayed a series of linked questions that scientists should ask themselves.

The first question is, did life start out as RNA? If the answer is no — and some scientists believe that to be the case — then they have to grapple with a different set of challenges to explain the origin of life.

For scientists who do accept an RNA-based origin of life, however, they need to find chemistry to produce it. Dr. Benner has one hypothesis. If scientists don't like it, then it's up to them to find an alternative — which other scientists are indeed doing.

And if you accept Dr. Benner's chemistry, then you have to find a place with oxygen and dry land where it can unfold. If the early Earth doesn't meet those standards, then we have to look elsewhere.

"That's the logic that drives you to Mars," said Dr. Benner.

Dr. Hazen, who invited Dr. Benner to deliver the lecture in Italy, said: "He made a good, logical case." He praised Dr. Benner's specific suggestions about what evidence geologists should be looking for to see which way we should travel down the logic tree.

Dr. Hazen, for one, is taking Dr. Benner up on the challenge to find evidence to test our ideas about the origin of life. He is now studying 3.8-billion-year-old rocks from Greenland, inside which are boron-laden minerals. If the boron once existed as borate in deserts — something Dr. Hazen doubts — then it may have left some clues behind in the rocks.

"I want to prove myself wrong before somebody else does," said Dr. Hazen.

If Dr. Hazen's research bears fruit, then Dr. Benner will happily abandon the idea that our ancestors started out on the Red Planet. "Then I have all the deserts I need. I don't have to go to Mars," he said.

In a Dome in Hawaii,
a Mission to Mars

BY KENNETH CHANG | OCT. 20, 2014

ON THE WAY TO MARS, Neil Scheibelhut stopped by Walmart for mouthwash and dental floss. "We're picking up some last-minute things," he said via cellphone last Wednesday afternoon from the store.

Mr. Scheibelhut is not actually an astronaut leaving the earth. But three hours later, he and five other people stepped into a dome-shaped building on a Hawaiian volcano where they will live for the next eight months, mimicking a stay on the surface of Mars.

This is part of a NASA-financed study, the Hawaii Space Exploration Analog and Simulation, or Hi-Seas for short. The goal is to examine how well a small group of people, isolated from civilization, can get along and work together.

When astronauts finally head toward Mars years from now — NASA has penciled the 2030s — it will be a long and lonely journey: about six months to Mars, 500 days on the planet, and then another six months home.

"Right now, the psychological risks are still not completely understood and not completely corrected for," said Kimberly Binsted, a professor of information and computer sciences at the University of Hawaii at Manoa and the principal investigator for the project. (She is not in the dome.) "NASA is not going to go until we solve this."

Isolation can lead to depression. Personality conflicts can spin out of control over the months.

"How do you select and support astronauts for a mission that will last two to three years in a way that will keep them healthy and performing well?" Dr. Binsted said. Or as Mr. Scheibelhut put it:

"I'm so interested to see how I react. 'I don't know' is the short answer. I think it could go a lot of different ways."

Several mock Mars missions have been conducted in recent years. A simulation in Russia in 2010 and 2011 stretched 520 days, most of the duration of an actual mission. Four of the six volunteers developed sleep disorders and became less productive as the experiment progressed. The Mars Society, a nonprofit group that promotes human spaceflight, has run short simulations in the Utah desert since 2001 and is looking to do a one-year simulation in the Canadian Arctic beginning in 2015.

Hi-Seas has already conducted two four-month missions, and next year, six more people will reside for one year inside the dome, a two-story building 36 feet in diameter with about 1,500 square feet of space. It sits in an abandoned quarry at an altitude of 8,000 feet on Mauna Loa.

To simulate the operational challenges, the crew members in the Hi-Seas dome are largely cut off. Their communications to the world outside the dome are limited to email, and each message is delayed by 20 minutes before being sent, simulating the lag for communications to travel from Mars to Earth and vice versa.

Every time one of the would-be astronauts or mission control sends a message, at least 40 minutes will elapse before a reply arrives. Real-time conversation is impossible.

On a real mission, the lag time would often be considerably shorter as Mars and Earth moved closer together, but Dr. Binsted said, "We went with the worst case because we're trying to solve the worst-case situation."

The crew members are granted some exceptions. They can check a few websites, like their banking accounts, to ensure that their earth lives do not fall apart while they are away. There is also a cellphone for emergency communications; If a hurricane (a distinctly un-Martian weather pattern) were to threaten the dome, as almost occurred over the weekend when Hurricane Ana veered south of Hawaii, mission control would not delay telling the crew to evacuate.

Some 150 people applied to participate. Dr. Binsted said the three men and three women of this Hi-Seas crew were chosen to have a similar mix of experience and backgrounds as real NASA astronauts, and many indeed aspire to go to space.

The commander is Martha Lenio, 34, an entrepreneur looking to start a renewable-energy consulting company. Other crew members are Jocelyn Dunn, 27, a Purdue University graduate student; Sophie Milam, 26, a graduate student at the University of Idaho; Allen Mirkadyrov, 35, a NASA aerospace engineer; and Zak Wilson, 28, a mechanical engineer who worked on military drone aircraft at General Atomics in San Diego.

"I dream about being an astronaut, and this might be the closest I ever get," Ms. Dunn said.

Mr. Wilson had previously done a two-week stay at the Mars habitat in Utah. Mr. Scheibelhut had worked on the first Hi-Seas mission as part of the ground support crew. "I thought it would be really cool to be part of what's going on inside," he said.

For their time, each is receiving round-trip airfare to Hawaii, a $11,500 stipend, food and, of course, lodging.

At the outset, the six appear to get along fine. "This is a fantastic group of people," Mr. Scheibelhut said. "Right now, everything is wonderful."

He said he recognized that there would be unpleasant patches. "Eight months — you're going to have real conflicts you're going to have to work out," he said. "Scientifically speaking, it's going to be really interesting to see what happens."

But Mr. Scheibelhut, 38, an Army veteran who served a year in Iraq in 2004, said, "I've been through worse."

On this mission, at least, no one will be trying to kill him. "I hope," he added.

The goal is to maintain cohesion among the crew members, but that too can lead to problems.

"They become more independent when they are more cohesive," Dr. Binsted said, and an independent-minded crew could start sparring with mission control.

The researchers will also be looking for signs of "third-quarter syndrome." At the beginning of the mission, the experience is new and exciting. Then, in the second quarter of the mission, people fall into routines. Near the end, people can look forward to getting out and returning to the real world.

In the middle, there can be a stretch when routines turn into tedium without end. "That third quarter can be a bit of a bummer," Dr. Binsted said.

Like real astronauts, the Hi-Seas crew will be busy performing various scientific work, including excursions outside the dome in spacesuits.

"If you're going to keep people in a can for eight months, you want to get as much science out of them as possible," Dr. Binsted said. "It also means NASA gets a lot of bang for their buck."

Part of the science includes data Ms. Dunn will collect for her doctoral thesis. "Not a lot of people get to shut out the world for eight months and work on their research," she said.

But first, there was the stop at Walmart.

Ms. Dunn bought a pair of slippers. "The ground level stays pretty cool," she said.

Mr. Wilson picked up super glue and workout shorts. Dr. Binsted bought some supplemental food supplies — hot sauce, powdered coconut milk and spinach wraps.

Elsewhere, Ms. Lenio, the commander, was shopping for a ukulele.

"We'll start a band," said Mr. Scheibelhut, who had brought his guitar.

Looking to Mars to Help Understand Changing Climates

BY DENNIS OVERBYE | DEC. 8, 2014

Ten thousand times a hundred thousand dusty years ago
Where now it stands the Plain of Gold did once my river flow.
It stroked the stones and spoke in tongues and splashed against my face,
Till ages rolled, the sun shone cold on this unholy place.

THAT WAS THE PLANET MARS as channeled by the folk singer and science writer Jonathan Eberhart in "Lament for a Red Planet."

Ever since the Italian astronomer Giovanni Schiaparelli thought he spied lines that he called "canali" on Mars in 1877, earthlings' romantic thoughts about our nearest cosmic neighbor have revolved around water and its possible consequence, Life as We Know It. We haven't found life on Mars, but decades of robotic exploration have indeed strengthened astronomers' convictions that rivers and perhaps even oceans once flowed on the red planet.

Today Mars is an arid, frigid desert, suggesting that the mother of all climate changes happened there, about four billion years ago or so. The question that haunts planetary scientists is why? And could it happen here?

"I think the short story is the atmosphere went away and the oceans froze but are still there, locked up in subsurface ice," said Chris McKay, an astrobiologist and Mars expert at NASA's Ames Research Center.

In September a new spacecraft known as Maven, the Mars Atmosphere and Volatile Evolution mission, swung into orbit around the planet. Its job is to get a longer answer to one part of the mysterious Martian climate change, namely where the planet's atmosphere went.

One idea is that it was sputtered away by radiation and particles from the sun, known as the solar wind. Maven was designed to test that theory by measuring how fast Mars is losing atmosphere today.

The results could help scientists determine what the atmosphere was like four billion years ago, and just how warm and wet the planet was.

"We're going to get some suggestive answers," said Bruce Jakosky, a University of Colorado professor and principal investigator for Maven.

The results could resonate beyond Mars or even our solar system, shedding light on the fickle habitability of exoplanets. Alien astronomers looking at our solar system with a good telescope four billion years ago might have concluded that Mars was a likely habitat for life. Now look at it.

"What we are learning about are planetary atmospheres in general," said David Brain, a Colorado astronomer and Maven team member. "It's really fascinating to think that the planet changed in such a large way."

Everybody agrees that Mars was once wetter, on the basis of two lines of evidence. The surface of the planet is crossed with features that resemble old river channels, like the tributaries and canyons that lead into Chryse Planitia, the Plain of Gold, an ancient crater 1,000 miles wide and a mile-and-a-half deep. And NASA's rovers have found minerals characteristic of watery environments, formed four billion years ago.

But answers on exactly how wet and warm Mars was — and for how long — depend on whom you talk to.

According to one camp, Mars back then had a thick atmosphere with enough carbon dioxide, the greenhouse gas looming big in Earth's future, to warm up the temperature and keep it there for the hundreds of millions of years it would have taken to carve the Martian river system. Others have suggested that phenomena like asteroid impacts or the tilting of Mars's poles could have produced shorter periods of near-freezing temperatures. The impact that created the huge crater called the Hellas basin, for example, would have hurled vast amounts of vaporized rock into the sky — leading to decades or centuries of hot rain and flash floods, said Brian Toon of the University of Colorado. It might have been followed perhaps by a lingering era of nearly freezing temperatures as clouds left over from the steam bath produced a mild greenhouse effect.

Some geologists question whether the complicated river systems on Mars could have been created in such relatively short episodes, but they admit a serious flaw in their alternative view of a long-lasting greenhouse atmosphere of carbon dioxide. Namely, where did it go?

"The holy grail of Mars," said Dr. Jakosky of the Maven team, is to find the carbonate deposits that should have formed from its atmosphere. "We haven't found them," he said.

Which is where the new Maven mission comes in. One of the most striking clues that something has happened on Mars has come from atmospheric measurements from previous probes. They have shown that the lighter forms, or isotopes, of elements like hydrogen, nitrogen and argon are strangely depleted by contrast with their abundance on Earth.

On Mars the ratio of heavy nitrogen, which has an extra neutron in its nucleus, to regular nitrogen is twice that of Earth. The same pattern goes for argon, which is Dr. Jakosky's favorite because it is chemically inert and can't disappear from the inventory except by being swept out of the atmosphere.

All told, Dr. Jakosky said, the isotopic ratios on Mars suggest that about 60 to 90 percent of the atoms that were once in the Martian atmosphere might have been lost to space.

"We know the mechanism by which it was lost, but we can't quantify it yet," he said.

The story goes something like this. Once upon a time, Mars had a magnetic field that, like Earth's, acted as an umbrella, deflecting the rain of energetic particles shed by the sun. Earth's field is generated by a dynamo, which in turn is powered by rising heat, convection in the planet's molten iron core. Once Mars cooled off, the dynamo and the magnetic field stopped and the solar wind began pecking away at Mars's atmosphere. Ultraviolet radiation from the sun would ionize atoms in the upper atmosphere, making them subject to forces from magnetic fields carried along in the solar wind, and they would slip away into space an atom or two at a time.

"A little bit every few hours," Dr. Brain of Colorado said, and "suddenly you can change an entire planet."

Eventually — with no atmosphere, no rain and none of the tectonic churning that keeps Earth's oceans refreshed — the Martian rivers and oceans, if any, would have been absorbed into the ground and frozen, said James Kasting, a geoscientist at Penn State. Indeed, orbiting spectrometers have detected the signature of water in the form of ice under the wasted and lonely red sands.

In September, after a 10-month trip from Earth and just in time to observe the effects of Comet Siding Spring pass by Mars, Maven began settling into a looping orbit around Mars, flying as close as 77 miles. Its instruments will observe the sun and solar wind; Mars's upper atmosphere, the pool from which escaping particles are drawn; and the particles themselves as they escape. By understanding how the atmosphere is reacting to the sun today, Dr. Jakosky said, scientists should be able to extrapolate and say how much of the Martian atmosphere has been removed to space over the eons.

If the amount lost is substantial — "a couple of bars of CO_2," he said, describing it in units of the atmospheric pressure on Earth — "would tell us that Mars must have been warmer in the past."

If losses are trivial, he said, that would spell death for the early greenhouse theory, and the great Martian arguments would continue.

Mars Shows Signs of Having Flowing Water, Possible Niches for Life, NASA Says

BY KENNETH CHANG | SEPT. 28, 2015

SCIENTISTS HAVE for the first time confirmed liquid water flowing on the surface of present-day Mars, a finding that will add to speculation that life, if it ever arose there, could persist now.

"This is tremendously exciting," James L. Green, the director of NASA's planetary science division, said during a news conference on Monday. "We haven't been able to answer the question, 'Does life exist beyond Earth?' But following the water is a critical element of that. We now have, I think, great opportunities in the right locations on Mars to thoroughly investigate that."

That represents a shift in tone for NASA, where officials have repeatedly played down the notion that the dusty and desolate landscape of Mars could be inhabited today.

But now, John M. Grunsfeld, NASA's associate administrator for science, talked of sending a spacecraft in the 2020s to one of these regions, perhaps with experiments to directly look for life.

"I can't imagine that it won't be a high priority with the scientific community," he said.

Although Mars had rivers, lakes and maybe even an ocean a few billion years ago, the modern moisture is modest — small patches of damp soil, not pools of standing water.

In a paper published in the journal Nature Geoscience, scientists identified waterlogged molecules — salts of a type known as perchlorates — on the surface in readings from orbit.

"That's a direct detection of water in the form of hydration of salts," said Alfred S. McEwen, a professor of planetary geology at the University of Arizona, the principal investigator of images from a high-resolution camera on NASA's Mars Reconnaissance Orbiter and one of the authors of the new paper. "There pretty much has to have been liquid water recently present to produce the hydrated salt."

By "recently," Dr. McEwen said he meant "days, something of that order."

Scientists have long known that large amounts of water remain — but frozen solid in the polar ice caps. There have been fleeting hints of recent liquid water, like fresh-looking gullies, but none have proved convincing.

In 2011, Dr. McEwen and colleagues discovered in photographs from the orbiter dark streaks descending along slopes of craters, canyons and mountains. The streaks lengthened during summer, faded as temperatures cooled, then reappeared the next year.

They named the streaks recurring slope lineae, or R.S.L.s, and many thousands of them have now been spotted. "It's really surprisingly extensive," Dr. McEwen said.

Scientists suspected that water played a critical role in the phenomenon, perhaps similar to the way concrete darkens when wet and returns to its original color when dry.

But that was just an educated guess.

Lujendra Ojha, a graduate student at the Georgia Institute of Technology, turned to an instrument on the orbiter that identifies types of molecules by which colors of light they absorb. But this instrument, a spectrometer, is not as sharp as the camera, making it hard to zoom in on readings from the narrow streaks, a few yards across at most.

"We had to come up with new techniques and novel ways to do analysis of the chemical signature," said Mr. Ojha, the lead author of the Nature Geoscience article.

The researchers were able to identify the telltale sign of a hydrated salt at four locations. In addition, the signs of the salt disappeared when the streaks faded. "It's very definitive there is some sort of liquid water," Mr. Ojha said.

Then other samples were heated to 320 degrees Fahrenheit to sterilize them. If microbes were generating the radioactive gases, then there should be no gas rising from the sterilized soil.

That, too, is what happened.

"The response on Mars is well within the responses from terrestrial soils," Dr. Levin said, "most closely the Arctic and Alaska."

But in the absence of organic molecules, other Viking scientists discounted the possibility of life. It was like claiming the existence of a city in a place lacking wood, steel, bricks or any other building materials.

Dr. Levin has proposed, again and again, sending another labeled release experiment to Mars, to no avail. NASA's 2020 rover will be able to catalog a wide variety of organic molecules, but carries nothing to look for life directly.

Dr. Levin may finally get his wish with ExoMars, a European rover scheduled to launch in 2020. He is working with one of the teams building one of ExoMars's instruments to see if it could be modified to incorporate the labeled release apparatus.

There is a bit of a race against time. Dr. Levin, the last surviving member of the Viking biology team, is 92. "All I have to do is last that long," he said.

Can the U.S. Really Get Astronauts to Mars by 2030?

BY KENNETH CHANG AND DANIEL VICTOR | OCT. 11, 2016

IN AN ESSAY published Tuesday on CNN's website, President Obama renewed his call for American astronauts to visit Mars.

"We have set a clear goal vital to the next chapter of America's story in space: sending humans to Mars by the 2030s and returning them safely to Earth, with the ultimate ambition to one day remain there for an extended time," he wrote.

The plan is not new: The president laid out the same goal in 2010 during a speech at NASA's Kennedy Space Center in Florida.

But the column on Tuesday, along with a joint blog post by senior White House and NASA officials, offered new details on how the United States expected to reach the red planet.

In August, NASA awarded contracts to six companies to develop habitats that could eventually sustain astronauts on deep-space missions like Mars. On Tuesday, John P. Holdren, the White House science adviser, and Charles F. Bolden Jr., the NASA administrator, announced that NASA would also allow private companies to hitch their own modules to the International Space Station.

In the next decade, the officials added, work aboard the space station will move into a stage in which new technologies will be tested in the stretch of space between Earth and the moon.

Still, plenty of challenges remain. Here are some answers to the most pressing questions.

IS TRAVEL TO MARS EVEN POSSIBLE?

Yes. For decades, a human mission to Mars has been regarded as difficult but doable, given enough time and money and a willingness to subject astronauts to risks like radiation during the long journey.

THEN WHY AREN'T WE THERE ALREADY?

In his article, President Obama quoted John Noble Wilford, the New York Times reporter who covered the Apollo moon landings in the 1960s and '70s. Mars tugs at the imagination "with a force mightier than gravity," Mr. Wilford wrote.

Wernher von Braun, the mastermind of Apollo, sketched out plans for reaching Mars, too. Back then, many people thought the journey would move from the moon to Mars in a decade or two.

But President Richard M. Nixon pared back NASA's grand ambitions, leaving just the space shuttle. Astronauts have not ventured beyond low-Earth orbit since 1972, when the crew of Apollo 17 returned home after a 12-day trip to the moon.

In 1989, on the 20th anniversary of the Apollo 11 moon landing, President George Bush announced an initiative to send astronauts back to the moon and then onward to Mars. When NASA came back with a plan that was rumored to cost half a trillion dollars over two to three decades, the initiative faded.

The main challenge is not technical; it is political and financial. If Congress was to provide steady funding for the next 20 years, NASA could probably finish the task. But changes in presidential administrations have generally led to re-examination and changes in NASA's marching orders.

Unlike the flush years at the height of the Apollo program, peaking at 4.4 percent of the federal budget in 1966, NASA's budget today is steady and comparatively small: The $19.3 billion for the space agency this year amounts to about 0.5 percent of federal spending.

WON'T SPACEX GET THERE SOONER?

At the International Astronautical Congress last month in Guadalajara, Mexico, Elon Musk, the chief executive of SpaceX, announced his architecture for a giant rocket and spaceship — what he called the Interplanetary Transport System — that would take colonists to Mars, 100 at a time. The trips could begin as soon as 2024, he said.

Mr. Musk was confident, but that was a highly optimistic timeline. His smaller, workhorse rocket, the Falcon 9, has had two catastrophic failures in the past two years. A larger rocket under development, the Falcon Heavy, is years behind schedule.

SpaceX still has to prove new technologies, like the ability to land big spacecraft on Mars. And Mr. Musk was vague about how his company would pay for all this. SpaceX is still fairly small in size and profits, and Mr. Musk conceded that he would need to rely on "a huge public-private partnership."

HAS NASA BEEN PREPARING FOR A TRIP TO MARS?

Yes, but the pace has been slow. NASA has never received a large infusion of money to pursue a trip to Mars. And while the destination has not changed, the details certainly have.

For the last couple years, NASA news releases, web pages and social media postings have been festooned with the #JourneyToMars hashtag, tying a multitude of projects to the long-term goal of sending astronauts to Mars.

In 2010, the Obama administration scuttled the rockets and crew capsule that were to have been part of the canceled Constellation program in favor of developing better technologies for space travel.

Members of Congress objected, particularly those from Texas and Florida, home to big NASA facilities.

The Orion crew capsule from the Constellation program was revived, and Congress instructed NASA to start work on the Space Launch System, a heavy-lift rocket similar to the one that would have been built for the moon.

The first launch of the Space Launch System, without a crew, is scheduled for late 2018. The second launch, with astronauts, would be at least three years later.

The space agency is only now filling in details of what it would like to do on subsequent deep-space missions between Earth and the moon, which it calls "the proving ground."

WHEN MIGHT THE WORK BEGIN IN EARNEST?

Operating the International Space Station costs NASA $3 billion to $4 billion a year. Ditching the station — which NASA plans to do in 2024 — would free up money to build the other big pieces for a human Mars mission.

Last year, a team at NASA's Jet Propulsion Laboratory presented a proposal on how the agency could get to Mars in the early 2030s with its existing budget, along with increases to keep pace with inflation.

It would not be enough for the astronauts to land on Mars, as a lander would be too expensive.

This year, engineers at Lockheed Martin, building upon the pieces that NASA is developing, offered a proposal to send a spacecraft into orbit around Mars by 2028. NASA officials are not yet convinced.

At the International Astronautical Congress meeting, William H. Gerstenmaier, NASA's associate administrator for human exploration and operations, said he expected NASA astronauts in orbit around Mars in the 2030s.

But a landing will not occur until the 2040s, he said.

Earthlings, Unite: Let's Go to Mars

OPINION | BY TIM KREIDER | DEC. 16, 2017

THE ISSUES Donald Trump and I can find to agree on are few. I know this makes us both sad. Some people mock him for gorging himself on multiple Big Macs and Filets-o-Fish, but this is actually my favorite thing about him. I understand he likes elephants. And as of Monday, it turns out we agree on a third thing: sending human beings back to the moon, and to Mars.

It's an insane proposal, of course, and I don't believe the president really means it any more than he means to build his wall — he has probably forgotten saying it already and will deny it if asked. I don't even think going back to the moon is a good idea, per se; there's not much there, unless there are any Easter-egg monoliths waiting for us. It doesn't make much sense as a jumping-off point for Mars or a training ground for deep-space travel, and to quote President Barack Obama: "I just have to say pretty bluntly here: We've been there before." No offense to the moon, but it's boring; it doesn't inspire anymore.

I also don't subscribe to Stephen Hawking's notion that we need to get off this planet and establish a viable human population elsewhere lest we go extinct. I tend to side with Kim Stanley Robinson, author of a trilogy about the colonization of Mars, who in his more recent book "Aurora" portrays the dream of extraterrestrial colonization as a dangerous escapist fantasy — dangerous because it lets us imagine that we have an out, that we can just ditch this planet after we've ruined it instead of grappling with the imminent, serious, possibly terminal problems here, the only homeworld we're ever going to get.

I don't support going to Mars for practical reasons at all. I think we should plan to go to Mars because it would be a healthy sign that we, as a civilization, are still planning for a future — that we intend to live.

Because right now, frankly, we're not acting as though we do. We're acting more the way a friend of mine did in the last year of his life: letting the mail pile up unopened, heaping garbage in the house, littering the floor with detritus, no longer bothering to turn over the calendar pages. He'd clearly decided, on some level, to die.

We're mostly hiding from the horrifying facts mounting ever more unavoidably around us, keeping ourselves zonked out on anything from Xanax to Oxy, immersed in the worlds of Warcraft or Westeros while the actual world is burning. Billionaires are building sumptuous bunkers instead of doing anything that would forestall the deluge or revolution they're barricading against. Mounting a mission to Mars would be bold and hopeful, a gesture of faith, like planning a vacation to Bali next year when you're battling cancer.

Ray Bradbury, author of another famous Mars book, called space travel our modern version of cathedral building: a vast, ambitious, multigenerational undertaking, a shared vision to work toward together as a culture. Right now, we don't have such a vision, or even a culture, for that matter — just a degrading, every-man-for-himself scramble for the last scraps of cash the 1 percent have overlooked, like one of those parking-lot contests where you have to keep your hand on a truck until everyone faints from exhaustion. We could use a worthier project.

Anytime NASA shows us photos of phantasmagoric storms on Jupiter or Saturn spectacularly backlit, some killjoy demands to know how many billion dollars it cost and why we couldn't have spent that money on some of our pressing problems here on Earth. I notice these citizens never seem to muster up the same fiscal outrage over the squandering of trillions to kill foreigners or lock up brown people. Something's gone out of us since we explored the last of Earth; maybe some heroic overreach like a Mars program would get us all out of our cultural funk and inspire us to take on other equally hubristic challenges, like saving the world from drowning.

It's hard to blame people for being demoralized these days, especially in America. It's depressing to live in a collapsing empire, and it can distort your sense of perspective. But empires rise and fall, and it's a mistake to get too sentimentally attached to any one of them. Civilization is the thing at stake now: humanity.

Apocalyptic fatalism is the same sort of lazy escapism as fantasies of hyperspace day trips to Rigel. Evangelicals who think it's O.K. to wreck this world because there's a better one waiting for us need to grow up; eco-warriors who gripe that Earth would be better off if human beings just exterminated themselves should get back on their meds. Silly and stupid and selfish though human beings inarguably are, I am, reluctantly, for them — for us — because so far as we know, we're it for consciousness in this universe, the only game in town. And we owe it to something more than just ourselves or even our progeny to survive.

If beauty is in the eye of the beholder, and human consciousness is extinguished, so is all beauty. The Alps will be cold stone again, the Orion nebula hot gas. And not just the beauty we apprehend but all that we've made: Beethoven and Coltrane, Leonardo and Kurosawa. Extinguished, too, our accumulated understanding of this universe — the whole human testament from Buddha to Newton — not to mention the achievements of the nameless geniuses who first tamed an animal, grew food or made a fire. If we kill ourselves off with our animal aggression or let ourselves die through callousness or greed, we will have betrayed those ancestors and countless descendants, and leave the universe blind and dumb again, unintelligible to itself. And then it'll have to start over. Probably with the raccoons.

Some friends of mine gave birth to a child last week, a boy named Max. There are days when I feel like another baby is about the last thing this planet needs, but one traditionally suspends cynicism on these occasions. I sent the new mother a quotation I found by Carl Sandburg: "A baby is God's opinion that life should go on." I hope someday, after she and you and I are all dead, Max might stand at the edge of the Valles Marineris, a canyon longer than America, or on the slope of Olympus Mons, a volcano 14 miles high, and look for the blue-white morning star he came from. And maybe take a moment to remember us, who came before him and helped get him there. And then turn to look outward, at Jupiter, at Saturn, and the stars.

TIM KREIDER is the author of "I Wrote This Book Because I Love You."

Life on Mars? Rover's Latest Discovery Puts It 'On the Table'

BY KENNETH CHANG | JUNE 7, 2018

The identification of organic molecules in rocks on the red planet does not necessarily point to life there, past or present, but does indicate that some of the building blocks were present.

SCIENTISTS FOR THE FIRST TIME have confidently identified on Mars a collection of carbon molecules used and produced by living organisms.

That does not prove that life has ever existed on Mars. The same carbon molecules, broadly classified as organic matter, also exist within meteorites that fall from space. They can also be produced in chemical reactions that do not involve biology.

But the discovery, published on Thursday by the journal Science, is a piece of the Mars puzzle that scientists have long been seeking. In 1976, NASA's two Viking landers conducted the first experiments searching for organic matter on Mars and appeared to come up empty.

"Now things are starting to make more sense," said Jennifer L. Eigenbrode, a biogeochemist at NASA's Goddard Space Flight Center in Greenbelt, Md., and lead author of the Science paper. "We still don't know the source of them, but they're there. They're not missing any more."

The data comes from NASA's Curiosity rover, which has been exploring a former lake bed within the 96-mile Gale Crater where it landed in 2012. The discovery shows that organic molecules can be preserved near the Martian surface, surviving the bombardment of radiation from the sun.

"It's very exciting for Mars geology and for the search for life," said Sanjeev Gupta, a professor of earth sciences at Imperial College London in England, who was a co-author on the paper.

A second paper in Science adds wrinkles in the Martian puzzle of methane — a simple molecule of one carbon and four hydrogen

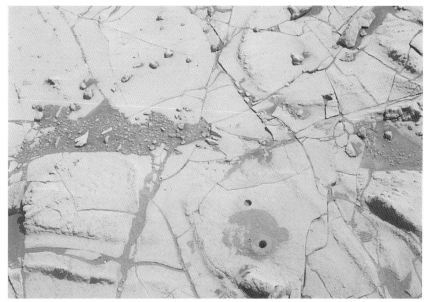

In 2015, the Curiosity rover drilled into a mudstone called "Mojave." Analysis of those drill cuttings yielded organic molecules.

atoms — that could also play an important part in figuring out whether life ever arose there and might even persist underground today.

The organic matter was found in pieces of solidified mud that Curiosity drilled into in 2015. The rocks formed about 3.5 billion years ago when Mars was drying out, although Gale Crater was still filled with water for stretches of thousands to millions of years.

The rock fragments were heated to more than 900 degrees Fahrenheit, and the rover's instruments looked at the molecules that wafted away at the high temperatures. Then the scientists sifted through the results to figure out what might be genuine Martian organics.

The analysis was complicated in part because a cup of solvent within the rover's mobile laboratory had leaked, contributing misleading signals. In addition, some of the readings could have come from contamination that had tagged along from Earth; others could have been produced in combustion as the sample was heated, which may have been the case in an earlier detection of organics by Curiosity.

"If we weren't sure, we removed it," Dr. Eigenbrode said.

In the end, a few smidgens of organics remained, including benzene and propane molecules.

"The detective work they did is worthy of Sherlock Holmes," said Katherine Freeman, a professor of geosciences at Pennsylvania State University who was not involved with the research. "What they show is that organics were present early on in Mars."

Intriguingly, the organics Dr. Eigenbrode and her colleagues detected looked like they were pieces that came from more complex material. The molecules could have come from something like kerogen, a component of fossil fuel that is found in coal and oil shale.

But the scientists cannot say what the larger molecules were or how they formed.

"We've considered three possible sources for the organics: geology, meteorites and biology," she said. When they did experiments in their laboratory on Earth to bake samples containing those three types of organic carbon, the readings were all consistent with what was detected on Mars.

That means they do not have compelling evidence for a biological origin of the carbon, but the possibility is not ruled out, either. "It's on the table with all the other ones," Dr. Eigenbrode said.

In the second Science paper, scientists led by Christopher R. Webster of the NASA Jet Propulsion Laboratory in Pasadena, Calif., find that levels of methane in the thin Martian atmosphere are usually very low, less than 0.5 parts per billion by volume. But with data now extending over five years, the scientists reported that methane levels go up and down by a factor of three, and the variations appear to follow Martian seasons.

"It's very, very fascinating and puzzling," Dr. Webster said.

Planetary scientists originally expected little methane in the Martian atmosphere, because that molecule is readily destroyed by sunlight and chemical reactions. But in 2003, observations from Earth indicated plumes of methane over parts of Mars. Those readings vanished two years later.

Because methane does not last in the atmosphere, any significant amounts there today must have been released recently. Methane can be created by geological interactions between rock, water and heat, or it could be a product of microbes that release methane as a waste product.

Curiosity added to the mystery when it looked for methane and initially didn't find any at all. A refined technique was able to measure lower levels, below 1 part per billion. Then in 2013 it recorded a burst of methane that lasted at least two months.

NASA

A self-portrait of Curiosity.

The rover has measured a few more methane spikes, but the new wrinkle is the undulations in the low background levels — higher in summer than winter. With the seasonal patterns, scientists can now begin to test ideas on the source of the methane, Dr. Webster said.

Michael J. Mumma, a scientist at the Goddard Space Flight Center who led earlier Earth-based measurements and who is not involved with the Curiosity research, said the work was carefully done and confirms the low background levels, but that he was not yet convinced of the seasonality of the variations.

He said his team has conducted another round of ground-based measurements earlier this year but they have not yet analyzed the data.

Additional information will come from the European Space Agency's Trace Gas Orbiter, which began its scientific data gathering a couple of months ago. Eventually, it will produce a global map of methane, but no results have been released yet.

Future missions could also provide additional clues to help scientists solve both the methane and organics puzzles. NASA's InSight spacecraft, currently en route, will measure marsquakes. It is possible that the impacts of meteors, which InSight might be able to record, rupture the surface and allow underground pockets of methane to rise into the atmosphere.

Two rovers launching in 2020, one from NASA and one from the European Space Agency, will also gather better rock samples to study organics. The European one will be able to drill a couple of yards into Martian rock, much deeper than the couple of inches that Curiosity was able to delve into.

The next NASA rover plans to collect rocks that will be brought back to Earth on a later mission where scientists will be able to examine them with a much wider array of instruments.

"Imagine what we can do on Earth in Earth laboratories in 10 years' time," Dr. Gupta said.

Glossary

Alpha Centauri A star system with identified exoplanets, the closest such star system to Earth at 4.37 light-years away.

Apollo program A human spaceflight program run by NASA from 1960 to 1972, which first landed astronauts on the moon in 1969.

asteroid A small, rocky body orbiting a star, ranging in size from that of a dust particle to that of a dwarf planet.

Cassini mission An international mission to send a space probe to Saturn between 1997 and 2017.

comet A small, icy body orbiting a star, known for releasing water and gases when it passes close to the star.

Enceladus A moon of Saturn's with oceans of liquid water under a sheet of ice.

exoplanet A planet outside of Earth's solar system.

flyby An observational space mission that passes a space object without entering its orbit.

gas planet A large, low-density planet consisting primarily of gases.

habitable zone An orbital region around a star where it is possible for liquid water to exist on a planet's surface.

hot Jupiter A gas planet with a very close orbit to its star, resulting in extremely high temperatures. Most of the earliest exoplanet discoveries were of this type.

Hubble Space Telescope A space telescope launched in 1990.

James Webb Space Telescope A space telescope, successor to Hubble and Kepler, planned for launch in 2021.

Kepler Space Telescope A space telescope launched in 2009, for the purpose of searching for exoplanets.

lander A spacecraft designed to land intact on an astronomical body.

light-year The distance traveled at the speed of light in one year, a common distance measure in astronomy.

main sequence star The most common star type in the universe, also known as a "dwarf star."

microbe A microscopic organism.

mini-Neptune A smaller gas planet, up to 10 Earth masses in size.

orbiter A space probe orbiting a planet.

probe A robotic spacecraft exploring astronomical bodies by visiting them in space.

rocky planet A planet similar in composition to Earth, containing primarily metals and silicates rather than gas.

rover A space exploration vehicle designed for locomotion on the surface of an astronomical body.

space shuttle program A NASA human spaceflight program from 1972 to 2011, which employed a reusable reentry vehicle.

spectrometer A tool that measures properties of astronomical bodies by measuring the spectrum of light they admit.

starshade A project in development that would help a space telescope search for Earth-like exoplanets by blocking unnecessary light.

super-Earth A rocky exoplanet type larger than Earth but too small to be a gas planet.

Trappist Acronym for the Transiting Planet and Planetesimals Small Telescope, located in Chile, which has discovered potentially habitable exoplanets.

Voyager 1 A still-operational space probe launched in 1977, the most distant man-made object in space.

Media Literacy Terms

"Media literacy" refers to the ability to access, understand, critically assess and create media. The following terms are important components of media literacy, and they will help you critically engage with the articles in this title.

angle The aspect of a news story that a journalist focuses on and develops.

attribution The method by which a source is identified or by which facts and information are assigned to the person who provided them.

balance Principle of journalism that both perspectives of an argument should be presented in a fair way.

bias A disposition of prejudice in favor of a certain idea, person or perspective.

byline Name of the writer, usually placed between the headline and the story.

chronological order Method of writing a story presenting the details of the story in the order in which they occurred.

credibility The quality of being trustworthy and believable, said of a journalistic source.

feature story Article designed to entertain as well as to inform.

headline Type, usually 18 point or larger, used to introduce a story.

human interest story Type of story that focuses on individuals and how events or issues affect their life, generally offering a sense of relatability to the reader.

impartiality Principle of journalism that a story should not reflect a journalist's bias and should contain balance.

intention The motive or reason behind something, such as the publication of a news story.

interview story Type of story in which the facts are gathered primarily by interviewing another person or persons.

inverted pyramid Method of writing a story using facts in order of importance, beginning with a lead and then gradually adding paragraphs in order of relevance from most interesting to least interesting.

motive The reason behind something, such as the publication of a news story or a source's perspective on an issue.

news story An article or style of expository writing that reports news, generally in a straightforward fashion and without editorial comment.

op-ed An opinion piece that reflects a prominent individual's opinion on a topic of interest.

paraphrase The summary of an individual's words, with attribution, rather than a direct quotation of their exact words.

quotation The use of an individual's exact words indicated by the use of quotation marks and proper attribution.

reliability The quality of being dependable and accurate, said of a journalistic source.

rhetorical device Technique in writing intending to persuade the reader or communicate a message from a certain perspective.

tone A manner of expression in writing or speech.

Media Literacy Questions

1. John Noble Wilford's article "In a Golden Age of Discovery, Far-away Worlds Beckon" (on page 10) is a long-form piece in seven parts. What is the purpose of each section?

2. Douglas Quenqua's article "Solar Systems With Their Own Rule Books" (on page 28) uses an inverted pyramid style of organization. Compare the first paragraph with the last. Why might the first be ranked higher in importance?

3. Adam Frank's op-ed "Yes, There Have Been Aliens," (on page 42) is immediately followed by Lisa Messeri's op-ed "What's So Special About Another Earth?" (on page 46). Compare the purpose of each of these op-eds. What are they trying to persuade the reader to believe?

4. Identify the angle of Kenneth Chang's article "For NASA, Longest Countdown Awaits" (on page 65). What aspect of NASA does it focus on?

5. Manoj Kumar Patairiya's article "Why India Is Going to Mars" (on page 71) includes human interest elements in its description of India's space program. What is the purpose of including these elements?

6. Sam Howe Verhovek's article "Not a Flight of Fancy" (on page 95) uses an analogy between the history of airplanes and space tourism as a rhetorical device. How does this device support Verhovek's argument about the necessity of space tourism?

7. Walter Isaacson's article "In This Space Race, Jeff Bezos and Elon Musk Are Competing to Take You There" (on page 113) is a book review. How is a book review different from a standard news article?

8. Sheila Marikar's article "The Rich Are Planning to Leave This Wretched Planet" (on page 119) conveys a distinctive tone in its headline and description of Axiom Space's plans for a commercial space station. How would you describe that tone?

9. Michael Roston's article "NASA's Next Horizon in Space" (on page 142) combines reporting with quotations and views submitted by experts and New York Times readers. How does the author work to achieve balance in the presentation of these views?

10. Dennis Overbye's article "Looking to Mars to Help Understand Changing Climates" (on page 177) begins with an epigraph, or quotation from a literary work. What is the purpose of this quotation?

11. Kenneth Chang's article "Visions of Life on Mars in Earth's Depths" (on page 186) uses paraphrased quotes of Gilbert V. Levin's controversial opinion that life on Mars has already been discovered. Does the paraphrase present these views without bias?

12. Tim Kreider's article "Earthlings, Unite: Let's Go to Mars" (on page 200) is an op-ed. What is the argument of this op-ed, and how is this argument made?

Citations

All citations in this list are formatted according to the Modern Language Association's (MLA) style guide.

BOOK CITATION

THE NEW YORK TIMES EDITORIAL STAFF. *Earth 2.0: The Search for a New Home.* New York: New York Times Educational Publishing, 2019.

ONLINE ARTICLE CITATIONS

ANGIER, NATALIE. "The Moon Comes Around Again." *The New York Times*, 7 Sept. 2014, https://www.nytimes.com/2014/09/09/science/revisiting -the-moon.html.

BAIDAWI, ADAM, AND KENNETH CHANG. "Elon Musk's Mars Vision: A One-Size-Fits-All Rocket. A Very Big One." *The New York Times*, 28 Sept. 2017, https://www.nytimes.com/2017/09/28/science/elon-musk-mars.html.

CHANG, KENNETH. "Asteroids and Adversaries: Challenging What NASA Knows About Space Rocks." *The New York Times*, 14 June 2018, https:// www.nytimes.com/2018/06/14/science/asteroids-nasa-nathan-myhrvold .html.

CHANG, KENNETH. "Astronomers Find Earthlike Planet, but It's Infernally Hot." *The New York Times*, 30 Oct. 2013, https://www.nytimes.com/2013 /10/31/science/space/astronomers-find-earthlike-planet-but-its-infernally -hot.html.

CHANG, KENNETH. "Elon Musk's Plan: Get Humans to Mars, and Beyond." *The New York Times*, 27 Sept. 2016, https://www.nytimes.com/2016/09/28 /science/elon-musk-spacex-mars-exploration.html.

CHANG, KENNETH. "For NASA, Longest Countdown Awaits." *The New York Times,* 24 Jan. 2011, https://www.nytimes.com/2011/01/25/science/space /25nasa.html.

CHANG, KENNETH. "In a Dome in Hawaii, a Mission to Mars." *The New York Times*, 20 Oct. 2014, https://www.nytimes.com/2014/10/21/science/taking -minds-on-a-journey-to-mars.html.

CHANG, KENNETH. "Life on Mars? Rover's Latest Discovery Puts It 'On the Table.' " *The New York Times*, 7 June 2018, https://www.nytimes.com /2018/06/07/science/mars-nasa-life.html.

CHANG, KENNETH. "Mars Shows Signs of Having Flowing Water, Possible Niches for Life, NASA Says." *The New York Times*, 28 Sept. 2015, https:// www.nytimes.com/2015/09/29/science/space/mars-life-liquid-water .html.

CHANG, KENNETH. "Meet SpaceX's First Moon Voyage Customer, Yusaku Maezawa." *The New York Times*, 17 Sept. 2018, https://www.nytimes.com /2018/09/17/science/spacex-moon-tourism-passenger.html.

CHANG, KENNETH. "Moon Express Sets Its Sights on Deliveries to the Moon and Beyond" *The New York Times*, 12 July 2017, https://www.nytimes.com /2017/07/12/science/moon-express-landers.html.

CHANG, KENNETH. "Philae Lander Nears a Cosmic Touchdown." *The New York Times*, 10 Nov. 2014, https://www.nytimes.com/2014/11/11/science /space/philae-lander-nears-a-cosmic-touchdown.html.

CHANG, KENNETH. "7 Earth-Size Planets Orbit Dwarf Star, NASA and European Astronomers Say." *The New York Times*, 22 Feb. 2017, https://www.nytimes.com/2017/02/22/science/trappist-1-exoplanets -nasa.html.

CHANG, KENNETH. "Space Council Chooses the Moon as Trump Administration Priority." *The New York Times*, 5 Oct. 2017, https://www.nytimes.com /2017/10/05/science/national-space-council-moon-pence.html.

CHANG, KENNETH. "Suddenly, It Seems, Water Is Everywhere in Solar System." *The New York Times*, 12 Mar. 2015, https://www.nytimes.com/2015 /03/13/science/space/suddenly-it-seems-water-is-everywhere-in-solar -system.html.

CHANG, KENNETH. "Venus: Inhospitable, and Perhaps Instructional." *The New York Times*, 17 Oct. 2016, https://www.nytimes.com/2016/10/18/science /venus-akatsuki-japan.html.

CHANG, KENNETH. "Virgin Galactic SpaceShipTwo Crash Traced to Co-Pilot Error." *The New York Times*, 28 July 2015, https://www.nytimes.com /2015/07/29/science/space/virgin-galactic-spaceshiptwo-crash-traced -to-co-pilot-error.html.

CHANG, KENNETH. "Visions of Life on Mars in Earth's Depths." *The New York Times,* 12 Sept. 2016, https://www.nytimes.com/2016/09/13/science/south -african-mine-life-on-mars.html.

CHANG, KENNETH, AND DANIEL VIKTOR. "Can the U.S. Really Get Astronauts to Mars by 2030?" *The New York Times*, 11 Oct. 2016, https://www.nytimes .com/2016/10/12/science/president-obama-nasa-mars.html.

DUFFY, JACK. "New Mission for American Aerospace Giants." *The New York Times*, 18 July 2010, https://www.nytimes.com/2010/07/19/business/global /19iht-ravspace.html.

FRANK, ADAM. "Yes, There Have Been Aliens." *The New York Times*, 10 June 2016, https://www.nytimes.com/2016/06/12/opinion/sunday/yes-there -have-been-aliens.html.

HARRIS, GARDINER. "On a Shoestring, India Sends Orbiter to Mars on Its First Try." *The New York Times,* 24 Sept. 2014, https://www.nytimes .com/2014/09/25/world/asia/on-a-shoestring-india-sends-orbiter-to -mars.html.

ISAACSON, WALTER. "In This Space Race, Jeff Bezos and Elon Musk Are Competing to Take You There." *The New York Times*, 24 Apr. 2018, https:// www.nytimes.com/2018/04/24/books/review/space-barons-christian -davenport-rocket-billionaires-tim-fernholz.html.

IVES, MIKE. "As America Looks Inward, China Looks to Outer Space." *The New York Times*, 23 May 2018, https://www.nytimes.com/2018/05/23/world /asia/china-space-moon.html.

KREIDER, TIM. "Earthlings, Unite: Let's Go to Mars." *The New York Times*, 16 Dec. 2017, https://www.nytimes.com/2017/12/16/opinion/sunday/lets -go-to-mars.html.

MARIKAR, SHEILA. "The Rich Are Planning to Leave This Wretched Planet." *The New York Times*, 9 June 2018, https://www.nytimes.com/2018/06/09 /style/axiom-space-travel.html.

MESSERI, LISA. "What's So Special About Another Earth?" *The New York Times*, 25 Aug. 2016, https://www.nytimes.com/2016/08/25/opinion/whats -so-special-about-another-earth.html.

OVERBYE, DENNIS. "Cassini Seeks Insights to Life in Plumes of Enceladus, Saturn's Icy Moon." *The New York Times*, 28 Oct. 2015, https://www .nytimes.com/2015/10/29/science/space/in-icy-breath-of-saturns-moon -enceladus-cassini-hunts-for-life.html.

OVERBYE, DENNIS. "Earth-Size Planets Among Final Tally of NASA's

Kepler Telescope." *The New York Times*, 19 June 2017, https://www.nytimes
.com/2017/06/19/science/kepler-planets-earth-like-census.html.

OVERBYE, DENNIS. "An Interstellar Visitor Both Familiar and Alien." *The New
York Times*, 22 Nov. 2017, https://www.nytimes.com/2017/11/22/science
/oumuamua-space-asteroid.html.

OVERBYE, DENNIS. "Looking to Mars to Help Understand Changing Climates."
T*The New York Times*, 8 Dec. 2014, https://www.nytimes.com/2014/12/09
/science/looking-to-mars-to-help-understand-changing-climates.html.

OVERBYE, DENNIS. "Meet TESS, Seeker of Alien Worlds." *The New York Times*,
26 Mar. 2018, https://www.nytimes.com/2018/03/26/science/tess-nasa
-exoplanets.html.

OVERBYE, DENNIS. "NASA Says Data Reveals an Earth-Like Planet,
Kepler 452b." *The New York Times*, 23 July 2015, https://www.nytimes
.com/2015/07/24/science/space/kepler-data-reveals-what-might-be-best
-goldilocks-planet-yet.html.

OVERBYE, DENNIS. "Reaching for the Stars, Across 4.37 Light-Years." *The New
York Times*, 12 Apr. 2016, https://www.nytimes.com/2016/04/13/science
/alpha-centauri-breakthrough-starshot-yuri-milner-stephen-hawking.html.

OVERBYE, DENNIS. "The Telescope of the 2030s." *The New York Times*, 13 July
2015, https://www.nytimes.com/2015/07/14/science/space/the-telescope
-of-the-2030s.html.

OVERBYE, DENNIS. "Telescope That 'Ate Astronomy' Is on Track to Replace
Hubble." *The New York Times*, 21 Nov. 2016, https://www.nytimes.com
/2016/11/22/science/nasa-webb-space-telescope-hubble.html.

PATAIRIYA, MANOJ KUMAR. "Why India Is Going to Mars." *The New York Times*,
22 Nov. 2013, https://www.nytimes.com/2013/11/23/opinion
/india-must-go-to-mars.html.

QUENQUA, DOUGLAS. "Solar Systems With Their Own Rule Books." *The New
York Times*, 9 Oct. 2014, https://www.nytimes.com/2014/10/14/science
/space/other-solar-systems-dont-play-by-our-rules.html.

ROSTON, MICHAEL. "NASA's Next Horizon in Space." *The New York Times*,
28 Aug. 2015, https://www.nytimes.com/interactive/2015/08/25/science
/space/nasa-next-mission.html.

VERHOVEK, SAM HOWE. "Not a Flight of Fancy." *The New York Times*,
3 Nov. 2014, https://www.nytimes.com/2014/11/04/opinion/space
-tourism-isnt-frivolous-or-impossible.html.

WILFORD, JOHN NOBLE. "In a Golden Age of Discovery, Faraway Worlds Beckon." *The New York Times*, 9 Feb. 1997, https://www.nytimes.com/1997/02/09/us/in-a-golden-age-of-discovery-faraway-worlds-beckon.html.

ZIMMER, CARL. "A Far-Flung Possibility for the Origin of Life." *The New York Times*, 12 Sept. 2013, https://www.nytimes.com/2013/09/12/science/space/a-far-flung-possibility-for-the-origin-of-life.html.

ZRAICK, KAREN. "NASA Names Astronauts for Boeing and SpaceX Flights to International Space Station." *The New York Times*, 3 Aug. 2018, https://www.nytimes.com/2018/08/03/science/nasa-astronauts-boeing-spacex.html.

Index

This book is current up until the time of printing. For the most up-to-date reporting, visit www.nytimes.com.